D1563292

W. B. YEATS AND THE CREATION OF A TRAGIC UNIVERSE

W. B. YEATS AND THE CREATION OF A TRAGIC UNIVERSE

Maeve Good

BARNES & NOBLE BOOKS
TOTOWA, NEW JERSEY

© Maeve Good 1987

First published in the USA 1987 by
BARNES & NOBLE BOOKS
81 ADAMS DRIVE
TOTOWA, NEW JERSEY, 07512

ISBN 0–389–20642–3

Printed in Hong Kong

Library of Congress Cataloguing-in-Publication Data
Good, Maeve.
W. B. Yeats and the creation of a tragic universe.
Bibliography: p.
Includes index.
1. Yeats, W. B. (William Butler), 1865–1939 – Dramatic works.
2. Yeats, W. B. (William Butler), 1865–1939.   Vision.
3. Tragedy.   4. Cuchulain (Legendary character) in literature.
I. Title.
PR5908.D7G66   1987   822'.8   86–10891
ISBN 0–389–20642–3

In memory of Stella

Contents

Acknowledgements

I am grateful to Michael B. Yeats and Macmillan London Ltd for permission to quote from the works of W. B. Yeats. In addition, extracts are reprinted with the kind permission of Macmillan Publishing Company (New York): from *Autobiographies* by W. B. Yeats (copyright 1916, 1936 by Macmillan Publishing Company, renewed 1944, 1964 by Bertha Georgie Yeats); from *Mythologies* by W. B. Yeats (copyright © 1959 by Mrs W. B. Yeats); from *A Vision* (copyright 1937 by W. B. Yeats, renewed 1965 by Bertha Georgie Yeats and Anne Butler Yeats); from *The Letters of W. B. Yeats*, edited by Allan Wade (copyright 1953, 1954 and renewed 1982 by Anne Butler Yeats); from *The Variorum Edition of the Poems of W. B. Yeats*, edited by Peter Allt and Russell K. Alspach (copyright 1957 by Macmillan Publishing Company); from *Essays and Introductions* (copyright Mrs W. B. Yeats 1961); from *Explorations* (copyright Mrs W. B. Yeats 1962); from *Collected Plays* by W. B. Yeats (copyright 1934, 1952 by Macmillan Publishing Company, renewed 1962 by Bertha Georgie Yeats, and 1980 by Anne Yeats); from *The Variorum Edition of the Plays* by W. B. Yeats, edited by Russell K. Alspach (copyright Russell K. Alspach and Bertha Georgie Yeats 1966; copyright © Macmillan & Co. Ltd 1965); from *Collected Poems* by W. B. Yeats (copyright 1912, 1916, 1919, 1924, 1928, 1933, 1934 by Macmillan Publishing Company, renewed 1940, 1944, 1947, 1952, 1956, 1961, 1962 by Bertha Georgie Yeats; copyright 1940 by Georgie Yeats, renewed 1968 by Bertha Georgie Yeats, Michael Butler Yeats and Anne Yeats).

List of Abbreviations

Page numbers for citations of Yeats's works are so far as possible given in the text. The abbreviations used, and the editions to which they refer, are as follows:

A   *Autobiographies* (London: Macmillan, 1955).

CP   *The Collected Poems of W. B. Yeats*, 2nd edn (London: Macmillan, 1950).

CPl   *The Collected Plays of W. B. Yeats*, 2nd edn (London: Macmillan, 1952).

E   *Explorations* (London: Macmillan, 1962).

E&I   *Essays and Introductions* (London: Macmillan, 1961).

L   *The Letters of W. B. Yeats*, ed. Allan Wade (London: Rupert Hart-Davis, 1954).

M   *Mythologies* (London: Macmillan, 1959).

V   *A Vision* (London: Macmillan, 1962). (First published 1937.)

VPl   *The Variorum Edition of the Plays of W. B. Yeats*, ed. Russell K. Alspach (London: Macmillan, 1966).

Introduction

In 1900 Yeats wrote of Shelley,

> a single vision would have come to him again and again, a
> vision of a boat drifting down a broad river between high hills
> where there were caves and towers, and following the light of
> one Star; . . . and voices would have told him how there is for
> every man some one scene, some one adventure, some one
> picture that is the image of his secret life . . . .
>
> <div align="right">(<i>E&I</i>, pp. 94–5)</div>

Shelley's single vision presents, in his poetry, a characteristic
landscape or imaginative frame of reference. In this study I trace
Yeats's creation of such a landscape and I argue that this landscape and the world system behind it are conceived as tragic. My
study explores Yeats's dance plays, the material which culminates in *A Vision* and Cuchulain, the hero who dominates Yeats's
world.

The typical landscape of this tragic world is the west of
Ireland, its barren terrain, stunted trees, storm-beaten towers,
waste land. In contrast to this are isolated images of delight:
gracious ancestral houses, fountains, dancers, great-rooted blos-
soming trees. The inhabitants of this tragic world are not all
human. Curlews, herons, hawks and the solitary swan imply
isolation and, frequently, desolation. The mythical Cuchulain
encounters Fand and the Sidhe. The Young Man of *The Dreaming
of the Bones* encounters ghosts. The human inhabitants of the
landscape are, like the sea-borne birds, almost always seen as
isolated, brought to ruin and destruction: Swift ending in madness, Parnell brought down by those he had served. They are
always in search of an impossible aim. Yeats's concept of tragedy
comes from a recognition of the inevitability of their defeat.

Behind these heroes and their landscape, Yeats constructs, in
A Vision, a system which ensures and to some extent explains the

necessity of defeat. From Yeats's system we learn that history is the opposite of progress. Yeats denies the absolute power of Christianity. We note his sense of each individual forced to choose a mask or mode of expression out of what confronts or terrifies him. The choosing of a mask, the confrontation with his terror, provides man with the only way of making the tragic gesture, but also the only way of making any coherent gesture or expression of himself:

> If we cannot imagine ourselves as different from what we are, and try to assume that second self, we cannot impose a discipline upon ourselves though we may accept one from others. Active virtue, as distinguished from the passive acceptance of a code, is therefore theatrical, consciously dramatic, the wearing of a mask.   (*M*, p. 334)

Yeats's hero, then, if he lives at all, cannot escape tragic conflict. He is an active protagonist with the dark, with all that he is not. As with Cuchulain, he is fighting the waves.

Yeats's creation of a tragic landscape is made coherent by the response which it evokes. Aristotle defines tragedy in terms of pity and fear; Yeats defines it in terms of terror and delight, what he calls the Vision of Evil and Unity of Being. Terror and the Vision of Evil dominate in Yeats's plays, culminating in the horror of *Purgatory*. In the poetry, too, terror is a frequent emotional response. In 'A Dialogue of Self and Soul', for example, terror is compounded with horror in both the imaginative–spiritual and human–bestial world. But we also find delight and joy. In Yeats, delight frequently springs from the accomplishment of style, the achievement of art against a backdrop of chaos. But in the poem we find that, like its opposite, delight lies in the affirmation of vitality, of human love. 'A blind man battering blind men' can find,

> When such as I cast out remorse
> So great a sweetness flows into the breast
> We must laugh and we must sing,
> We are blest by everything,
> Everything we look upon is blessed.
>
> (*CP*, p. 267)

The polarities are utterly dependent on each other. Yeats's vision springs partly from the Blakean concept, 'Pity would be no more / If we did not make somebody Poor'.[1] If a world existed in which all were strong, beautiful and brave, then the concepts of strength, beauty and valour would no longer have meaning. Tragedy arises from the recognition of an irremediable state of affairs. The only achievement possible in a tragic world is the enactment of tragic conflict. A passage from *Autobiographies* states the central truth of the tragic situation as seen by Yeats. The tragic masters

> would not, when they speak through their art, change their luck; yet they are mirrored in all the suffering of desire. The two halves of their nature are so completely joined that they seem to labour for their objects, and yet to desire whatever happens, being at the same instant predestinate and free.
>
> (p. 273)

One cannot then, choose the tragic, only recognise it as Yeats does in 'The Cold Heaven', when 'Suddenly I saw the cold and rook-delighting heaven' (*CP*, p. 140). For Yeats this means a recognition of his place in a never-ending cycle of tragic endeavour:

> I declare this tower is my symbol; I declare
> This winding, gyring, spiring treadmill of a stair
>   is my ancestral stair.
>
> (*CP*, p. 268)

Yeats's creation in his art of a tragic universe gives rise to several critical problems. For example, his rejection of Christianity and the salvation it offers – in favour of a cyclical system of never-ending conflict – forces us to look closely at Yeats's definition of such concepts as evil, good, innocence and responsibility.

Yeats's response to violence and calamity is involved here. Then, the construction of such an arbitrary and harsh system as that in *A Vision* can seem an inadequate representation of human life. Yeats sometimes appears to indulge in brutality, presenting a sensational horror story of blood and mire and a perversion of instinct where sexual love, for example, is made grotesque:

> A bastard that a pedlar got
> Upon a tinker's daughter in a ditch.
>   (*CPl*, p. 684)

I argue that these problems result partly from a misunderstanding of the nature of tragedy. In this context I take issue with two critical responses to Yeats's tragic world. The first, most coherently argued by Helen Vendler in *Yeats's 'Vision' and the Later Plays*,[2] is enlightening in its exploration of Yeats's aesthetics, his study of the process of poetic composition, inspiration, the reordering of disparate experience into an articulate whole. But this view tends to ignore any tragic dimension. In addition, Helen Vendler refuses to confront Yeats's redefinition of evil and does not allow its presence in Yeats's thinking. Another response with which I take issue is twofold. It regards tragedy as outmoded in the twentieth century, but also as barbaric. Tragedy's concentration on the heroic does not assort comfortably with a democratic world, while the characteristic tragic gesture of death may seem extravagant. Balachandra Rajan, in a perceptive essay, 'Synge, Yeats and the Tragic Understanding', writes on twentieth-century implications for tragedy:

> To think of character isolated by a deed is to recognise that the tragic deed must be death and that death is not simply the bridegroom and the skeleton but the hero's culminating announcement of himself. . . . The formal statement of that alienation is that too high a price is being paid for poetry when we actually listen to what the poet has to say.[3]

Rajan argues that this gesture, the hero's act of self-realisation, becomes more subtle. It is 'the statement of dignity',[4] a 'superior work of art, a poem capable of passing into myth'.[5] Writing of Yeats's *Deirdre*, he outlines the perils facing tragedy: 'The perils that she faces are that she may die shabbily rather than expressively, or that she may not be permitted to die at all.'[6] He argues that death 'in the grand style'[7] is a gesture almost fully exhausted, that tragedy must move within tightening constrictions. It becomes 'creative defiance'[8] and can only be achieved, he argues, through an accommodation with the comic: 'nobility and absurdity . . . interwoven into the garment of life'.[9]

Tragedy may be regarded not simply as outmoded in the twentieth century, but as inadmissable, reprehensible and positively evil in its destructive waste. Harold Bloom, in his study *Yeats*,[10] frequently attacks Yeats for his brutality and anti-human stance. But this attack, I argue, is finally an attack on tragedy itself, an attack on a pessimistic stance which rejects working towards a better world. I argue that Yeats's presentation of the tragic concentrates on this dark element in the tragic world, on its terror. The critic Jan Kott, in *The Eating of the Gods*, illustrates the essentially bleak nature of tragedy. As with Rajan, the emphasis is on the gesture of death:

> In the tragic world the dead return. The tragic hero is alone among people, perhaps because he lives like Antigone, in the world of the dead, in the world of those who have been murdered, or whom he has murdered himself. . . . The succeeding generations must satisfy the demands of the dead, give meaning to their death and restore justice to the world. But this mediation through time only ends in tragedy, with new corpses filling the stage. The dead eat the living.[11]

Kott describes tragedy as an attempt to justify suffering. The hero is a scapegoat, a figure of mediation:

> The tragic opposition exists between suffering which does not justify anything and myth which justifies all . . . there takes place a transformation of the cruel god into the just God and of time which devours everything into history achieving its aim.[12]

What differentiates this transformation from a Christian viewpoint is that it is hopeless, its pattern always repeated: 'Tragedy is an appeal for mediation and at the same time a demonstration of the impossibility of such mediation.'[13] With one reservation this is Yeats's world. We recognise *Purgatory*:

> O God,
> Release my mother's soul from its dream!
> Mankind can do no more. Appease
> The misery of the living and the remorse of the dead.
> (*CPl*, p. 689)

The one reservation I suggest is that Yeats does not attempt to justify suffering. In fact he does not attempt to justify anything. He perceives the situation as hopeless. He is 'satisfied' (*VPl*, p. 935) with its drama.

The other side of Yeats's tragic world, delight or Unity of Being (see *V*, p. 82), does break through in momentary flashes of brilliance:

> What motion of the sun or stream
> Or eyelid shot the gleam
> That pierced my body through?
> What made me live like these that seem
> Self-born, born anew?
>
> (*CP*, p. 289)

But the tragic world turns away from permanent delight. Murray Krieger in *The Tragic Vision* offers a helpful context in which to view both the dark and the light side of tragedy in the twentieth century and in Yeats. Where Rajan suggested a narrowing of the tragic field, Krieger sees the tragic understanding as an engulfing force. He distinguishes between the terms 'tragedy' and 'tragic vision':

> The most obvious difference I would mark between the two is also a crucial one: 'tragedy' refers to an object's literary form, 'the tragic vision' to a subject's psychology, his view and version of reality. It is more than a difference between two extant approaches to the tragic. Rather, the second has usurped the very possibility of the first after having been born side by side with it. Perhaps it would be more accurate to say that the tragic vision was born *inside* tragedy, as a part of it. . . . But fearful and demoniac in its revelations, the vision needed the ultimate soothing power of the aesthetic form which contained it – of tragedy itself – in order to preserve for the world a sanity which the vision itself denied.[14]

After outlining the growth of the modern hero, whom he sees typified in the figure of Conrad's Kurtz with his recognition of horror as the central truth, Krieger returns to the classic vision which he sees as inclusive. It was, he argues, a vision of the world, without being crass, that is universal and conducive to order without optimistically thinning moral reality . . . . This vision is the all-embracing one of an older world and an older order. It is what I have tried to talk about in discussing the formal and thematic triumph of tragedy over the errant tragic vision it contained within it. It is as if the security of the older order wanted to test the profundity of its assurances, its capacity to account for the whole of human experience, and thus bred within itself the tragic vision as its *agent provocateur*. . . . Consequently, it can witness all that befalls its hero without sharing in his disavowal of the meaning of our moral life; without denying with him, the sensibleness of the universe and of life despite the explosive terrors they hold in store.[15]

Krieger argues that our world vision is no longer inclusive. We have no reference to a higher order. Yeats's explorations of those 'explosive terrors', his understanding of evil, are balanced by his concern with form, with images of coherence and beauty, 'a perfectly proportioned human body' (*V*, p. 82) – his emblem for Unity of Being, joy, delight and the soul. The balance is delicate. Yeats concentrates on the tension between the two, on their conflict. But the dark side, the Vision of Evil, is always threatening to break through.

This study begins with an exploration of Yeats's treatment of Cuchulain as the archetypal hero. We shall look at Yeats's response to the work of Ferguson and Lady Gregory in this context. Yeats's early response to Cuchulain is complicated by an interest in folk literature. From the start Yeats associates both the legends of Cuchulain and the stories of folk literature as being part of a shared world which constantly fuses the heroic or epic with the lyrical. There is a preoccupation with the supernatural. These legends and tales present an extension of reality rather than a mere reflection. In addition Irish legends and tales are firmly rooted in particular landscapes. Yeats suggests that place may be a way of opening a door into another world, that landscape is in fact visionary.

Against this background we explore the figure of the hero. Most characteristic of the hero is the death–feat, the celebration of heroic death and violent confrontation. While the hero is uncompromising, Yeats's treatment of the heroic is far from straightforward. Yeats's Cuchulain is simple, but constantly opposed by complexity, deception and subtlety. These forces are personified by the supernatural figures of the Sidhe, but also by a surface world increasingly hostile to the heroic temperament. Cuchulain is at war both with himself and with his milieu.

An exploration of Yeats's Cuchulain involves us in an exploration of Yeats's dramatic techniques. In the first decade of the twentieth century Yeats declares his dissatisfaction with conven-. tional and naturalistic techniques as a means of presenting the heroic. Gradually the idiosyncrasy of character is eliminated in favour of personality and archetype. Cuchulain is *the* hero rather than *a* hero. He is an archetypal expression of the heroic and we are asked to identify ourselves in him, to create him in our own minds. More and more we find that the hero himself is the key to revelation, to recognition of the tragic moment.

In Chapter 2 I explore three of Yeats's dance plays. In the first two, *At the Hawk's Well* and *The Only Jealousy of Emer*, we see Cuchulain in a new context, but one towards which we have seen Yeats working. The plays concentrate on vision, the participation of the audience in the construction of the tragic encounter, and on landscape. The structure of these plays presents a tightly knit unity in which hero, setting and audience are united in discovery. We are swept out of the everyday world into a fuller existence, a deeper knowledge. This is largely a knowledge of failure, bitterness and frustration. The landscape in which the plays are set becomes the objective embodiment of this emotion of loss. Yet the futility is part of the process towards vision. In *The Dreaming of the Bones* we leave Cuchulain. The journey of discovery is one we take ourselves, largely through the medium of the Young Man who is our guide, despite the limitations of his perception. In this play Yeats's discovery of the conventions of the Japanese Noh theatre reaches its climax and the use of chorus, mask and dance in conjunction with the landscape of frustration are fully integrated. This play explores the moment of tragic confrontation and establishes a characteristic landscape for the tragic moment which remains as a touchstone throughout Yeats's work. Finally, these dance plays are written as Yeats works towards *A Vision*. They explore facets of that vision.

In Chapter 3 we turn from the landscape of tragedy to the universe or world system which lies behind it. I attempt an overall view of Yeats's system. I aim to explore Yeats's *A Vision* in the context of his poetry and plays. I see it as a framework which Yeats has established to order his perceptions. It is not, I feel, in any way sufficient in itself, but it provides a map or an outline, with its phases of the moon, to which Yeats refers us.

From the framework of *A Vision* I return, in Chapter 4, to drama, exploring four of Yeats's later plays. *Calvary* and *The Resurrection* are concerned with the cyclical treatment of history as explored in *A Vision*. These plays reflect Yeats's dissatisfactions with Christianity, with the idea of any ultimate salvation. We are forced to redefine morality and to look closely at Yeats's definition of evil in this context. *The Words upon the Window-Pane* and *Purgatory* are concerned less with definition than with experience of this Vision of Evil. The sense of evil gathers momentum in these plays. All human life appears as degrading and horrific. But, against the figure of Swift grown mad and the Old Man of *Purgatory*, I shall draw attention to the figure of Oedipus. Oedipus balances the figure of Christ in the first two plays, but he also resembles the protagonists of the latter. These are, I would argue, a partial expression of his creative rage. All four plays are concerned with vision, revelation or apocalypse, and I see the dark world revealed in *Purgatory* as leading directly on to Yeats's final statements in *Last Poems* with their frequently savage expression of joy.

In conclusion I examine *The Death of Cuchulain* as the focal point for a summing-up of the tragic world presented by Yeats. Here again we are brought to vision, self-recognition. But, after the fury experienced not only in Cuchulain's tempestuous life, but also in so many of Yeats's poems, this final revelation is 'passing strange' in its quietness.

1 Cuchulain and the Sidhe: Vision and Tragic Encounter

Yeats's life closes with *The Death of Cuchulain*. He is the subject of one of the final meditations on death, 'Cuchulain Comforted'. He has the last word: 'No body like / His body has modern woman borne' (*CPl*, p. 705). He is finally synonymous with the Irish nation as its *alter ego* or ideal self. Cuchulain is an obsession with Yeats from the close of the nineteenth century and he survives to the end as the heroic archetype. Yeats's celebration of the heroic includes Swift, Tone, Parnell and, to an extent, Pearse; but it is Swift and Cuchulain who are most clearly and passionately delineated, Swift (discussed in Chapter 4) representative of passionate intellectual integrity, Cuchulain of heroic strength.

Since Yeats's concern with Cuchulain spans almost his entire career, Yeats's attitude and presentation of the hero necessarily alters and develops. With few exceptions Yeats presents Cuchulain through drama, and his experiments with different dramatic techniques are therefore crucial in our response to Cuchulain's role and our understanding of his significance. The 1916 Easter Rising is equally crucial. The cult of Cuchulain, so literally expressed in the Rising, corroborates Yeats's response to Cuchulain as the central Irish myth. But Yeats's response to this use of the myth is not fully articulated until *Last Poems* and the final play. In *At the Hawk's Well* of 1917 and *The Only Jealousy of Emer* of 1919, for example, Yeats's pursuit of the Cuchulain legends is largely unaffected by these events. Cuchulain in these plays is given highly individual esoteric treatment. After this there is silence on the subject of Cuchulain until the rewriting of *The Only Jealousy of Emer* as *Fighting the Waves* in 1929. Only when Yeats returns to complete the cycle with *The Death of Cuchulain*

11

and in *Last Poems* are we asked to confront the myth of Cuchulain in terms of the 1916 Rising. This time-lag is justified, for the significance of such events as those of 1916 can only be understood fully in retrospect; while bitter experience of civil war and the development of the new state in ways inimical to the poet determine that Yeats's final treatment of Cuchulain will be complex and ironic. To explore Yeats's concern with Cuchulain throughout his career also allows us to trace Yeats's development as a writer and to decipher the overall coherence of his work. Indeed Yeats's return to Cuchulain in his last play seems a highly conscious act, a deliberate restatement, a last word on the role and significance of the hero. Because of this deliberate use of Cuchulain and because of the long silence, there is a dissonance between the last play and those preceding it. It belongs to another chapter and I discuss the play in my conclusion.

This is, however, not the only dissonance we meet in Yeats's cycle. *On Baile's Strand* differs significantly from the dance plays *At the Hawk's Well* and *The Only Jealousy of Emer*, while *The Green Helmet* is the only play in which Yeats gives significant attention to the chivalric elements of the heroic code. His usual model for *courtoisie* is the Renaissance world of Castiglione. But though *On Baile's Strand* and *The Green Helmet* are different in technique from the two dance plays, both, particularly *On Baile's Strand*, show a hunger for a new form of presentation and dissatisfaction with naturalistic methods. Yeats's search for a new mode of presentation is central to his definition of the tragic and heroic. I argue that this definition is almost without exception unconventional and unexpected. From the very beginning Cuchulain is presented to us not so much as the powerful, victorious, self-assured warrior that we might expect. Rather he is shown to be bewildered, baffled and, at times, almost impotent. More predictable versions of the heroic are found in *The King's Threshold* or *Deirdre*, while *Cathleen ni Houlihan* is a much more obvious reflection of the heroic in relation to Ireland.

What distinguishes Yeats's treatment of Cuchulain from his treatment of the heroic in these plays is a question of emphasis. In them Yeats draws a simple opposition between good and evil, heroic and despicable, exceptional and common. With the figure of Cuchulain, however, Yeats does not simply emphasise the hero's opposition to external forces. He penetrates within the hero's personality. Two battles are being fought. First, there is a battle against a world hostile to the heroic temperament. Seen in this context heroism may appear as futile, irrelevant or simply barbarous. Secondly, Yeats focuses on Cuchulain's battle with a supernatural world. This battle is, at its simplest, a battle with destiny. Cuchulain's choice of a short life but a famed one leads him irrevocably to his final confrontation with death. Significantly, Cuchulain, whose heroic ethos is by definition simple, free, open and literally straightforward, is confronted by his opposite, by complexity and deception, a world in which his code of behaviour can only fail. He is fighting the sea, his 'sword against the thunder' (*CPL*, p. 276). His stature, however, is determined by his adherence to that code whatever faces him. *A Vision* tells us that the heroic nature 'is conscious of the most extreme degree of *deception*, and is wrought to a frenzy of desire for truth of self' (p. 127). Cuchulain's truth is his own death and each of his encounters explores facets of that death. The irony facing Cuchulain is that the world of deception and mystery is his true destiny. Overall in the cycle and within each play, Cuchulain moves from a twilit atmosphere into clarity or recognition of this truth.

Yeats's exploration of the tragic encounter focuses on vision or recognition. The development of new techniques – mask, dance and chorus – to convey this visionary encounter creates a landscape which embodies the emotional atmosphere of conflict. Indeed, in the dance plays (examined in Chapter 2) atmosphere and landscape dominate to the extent that they may even be said to dwarf the tragic hero at their centre. The landscape is the expression of the hostile world in which the hero is trapped. Yeats's techniques, as they develop from *On Baile's Strand* to the dance plays, impel the audience to create the heroic for themselves, to participate in the construction of the encounter on the stage and so to identify in Cuchulain 'the reality that is in our own minds' (*E*, p. 167). In this way Cuchulain becomes a vehicle for the vision of an inner self. He is type rather than character, personality in its fullest and therefore universal expression. Something of this insight is present in Yeats's Preface to *Cuchulain of Muirthemne*, where he argues,

the Irish stories make us understand why the Greek call myths the activities of the daemons. The great virtues, the great joys, the great privations come in the myths and, as it were, take mankind between their naked arms, and without putting off their divinity.[1]

In this chapter we follow the transformation of Cuchulain from characteristic heroic bravado into a state akin to trance, into an intense and rarefied visionary world.

Yeats's early response to Cuchulain, inspired largely by the work of Ferguson, O'Grady and finally Lady Gregory, finds expression long before the hero had been articulated as the presence summoned to the General Post Office in 1916. Nevertheless from the start Yeats associates him with 'National sentiment'.[2] In 1886 Yeats writes of the heroic cult, principally in relation to Cuchulain, in two related essays on Samuel Ferguson. Ferguson is 'the most central and most Celtic'[3] of the Irish writers precisely because he turns to ancient legends, to the heroic tradition. Slanders made against the Irish in which they are presented as 'men of infirm will and lavish lips'[4] are refuted. Instead Irish legends reveal the national character as obdurate, 'The mind of the Celt loves to linger on images of persistence; implacable hate, implacable love.'[5] But Yeat's response to this national characteristic goes beyond its diehard nature. In another essay written in 1886, also on Ferguson, he defines the heroic:

> Heroic poetry is a phantom finger swept over all the strings, arousing from man's whole nature a song of answering harmony. It is the poetry of action, for such alone can rouse the whole nature of man. It touches all the strings – those of wonder and pity, of fear and joy. It ignores morals, for its business is not in any way to make us rules for life, but to make a character. It is . . . a fire in the spirit, burning away what is mean and deepening what is shallow.[6]

This definition, with its tendency towards hyperbole and its echoes of Shelley, isolates three elements of the heroic towards which Yeats's response remains constant. First, it rouses the whole nature of man, his full personality and expression; secondly, it is outside a conventional morality; and, thirdly, it identifies the heroic with the ecstatic, 'a fire in the spirit'. Two other elements of heroic literature to which Yeats draws atten-

tion in these essays should be mentioned. First, Yeats stresses
'the continual introduction of the supernatural'.[7] This predilec-
tion for what is 'strange and fantastic'[8] is integral both to the
traditional legends of Cuchulain and to Yeats's treatment of
him. Secondly, we might note that Ferguson's 'Congal' provides
Yeats with some of the material he uses finally in *The Death of
Cuchulain*. It is Congal rather than Cuchulain who meets his
death at the hands of an idiot boy and a coward. 'Ah, strange
irony of the Celt!'[9] comments Yeats in 1886. Although more than
fifty years separates this perception from the final play, the
strange and the fantastic are set in motion from the beginning.

Yeats's first direct response to Cuchulain emerges with the
poem 'Cuchulain's Fight with the Sea' (*CP*, pp. 37–40), from
The Rose of 1893. Helen Vendler comments, 'Three times in his
life Yeats wrote about the death of Cuchulain',[10] the first being
this poem, which, she points out, was first conceived as a
death-poem. She continues, 'It is no accident that Cuchulain's
death interested Yeats so early, since the death of the epic hero is
always, from one point of view, the climax of the saga'[11] and she
argues that Cuchulain's killing of his son does, in any case, mark
the beginning of the end.[12] In Yeats's poem it is Emer, and not
Aoife, who is the mother of Cuchulain's son. Yet she is made to
fill something of the same role later filled by Aoife and the Sidhe.
She is identified with jealousy, but also with the retribution of
destiny. She is three times identified with blood. First she is
'raddling', dyeing her clothes the colour of blood; then she
herself is tainted, 'all raddled with the dye'; and, finally, she
strikes the messenger with 'raddled fist'. The conflict in this
poem is simpler than that we meet in *On Baile's Strand*. It is a
conflict between father and son, brought about by the con-
straints of the heroic tradition, for both are bound by oath and
are thus caught in a web of chance and choice. Cuchulain is
further deluded by the druid's magic. Deluded by Emer, deluded
by Conchubar, he is finally lured against the invulnerable tide.
But the tide is the appropriate antagonist for his unappeasable
sorrow. Yeats's style, too, is appropriate to this atmosphere of
delusion and defeat. Conchubar warns and commands,

> Cuchulain will dwell there and brood
> For three days more in dreadful quietude

> And then arise, and raving slay us all.
> Chaunt in his ears delusions magical,
> That he may fight the horses of the sea.

The word 'chaunt' serves to deepen the dream-like atmosphere
in which Cuchulain is submerged and manipulated:

> Cuchulain stirred,
> Stared on the horses of the sea, and heard
> The cars of battle and his own name cried,
> And fought with the invulnerable tide.

The style is as far removed as possible from the twentieth-
century epilogue to *The Death of Cuchulain*, but it is nevertheless
wholly typical of the way in which Cuchulain, the hero, is
bewildered first by magic and charms, by the supernatural
figures of the Sidhe, then by the complexities of a modern state,
and, finally, by the intervention of a hostile twentieth-century
world.

Yeats's concentration on the supernatural is pursued throughout the 1890s in his explorations of folklore. Fairies, ghosts and
bizarre animals fill the pages of *The Celtic Twilight*.[13] Yeats sees
heroic legend and folktale as part of a shared tradition. Folktales 'ascend like mediaeval genealogies through unbroken dig-
nities to the beginning of the world'.[14] This is the tradition or the
soil 'where all great art is rooted'.[15] Commenting on stories
collected by Douglas Hyde he concludes, 'such stories are not a
criticism of life but rather an extension. . . . They are as existence and not a thought, and make our world of tea-tables seem
but a shabby penumbra.[16]

The world of appearances is reversed and a war against
naturalism is launched. In his Preface to Lady Gregory's *Cuchulain of Muirthemne*[17] Yeats concentrates on this element in heroic
literature. It is not sundered from the folk tradition. Heroic
literature is abundant in what may 'seem at first irrelevant
invention'.[18] It constantly digresses, is full of 'lyrical outbursts'
and 'enigmatical symbols'.[19] It is 'half-epical, half-lyrical'.[20]
Throughout is evident 'a supernatural sanction',[21] an escape from
'daily circumstance',[22] an emphasis on momentary glimpses of
unearthly beauty and ecstatic emotion revealed through magical
transformations: '[a] moving world of cloaks made out of the

fleeces of Manannan; of armed men who change themselves into sea-birds; of goddesses who become crows; of trees that bear fruit and flower at the same time'.[23]

This literature created, 'for learned and unlearned alike', 'a communion of heroes, a cloud of stalwart witnesses'[24] to which the landscape is a key. Yeats recognises local Irish landscapes as the setting for these encounters with figures from another world, for 'they lived in the places where we ride and go marketing'.[25] In *Autobiographies* Yeats sees a literature and a culture bound to place as far-reaching in their implications:

> Perhaps even these images, once created and associated with river and mountain, might move of themselves and with some powerful, even turbulent life, like those painted horses that trampled the rice fields of Japan.   (p. 194)

Yeats is bent on creating a visionary landscape. What is important here is to note that Yeats singles out from heroic literature its digressions. His interest in the heroic centres on the supernatural element, the existence of another world or dimension to which heroic action may lead us. He concentrates, too, on landscape as a key to this encounter. Ordinary perceptions are reversed. Images or spirits may transform our world. His interest is in transformation and discovery. The brave deeds of fighting men sometimes take second place.

In essays of 1903 and 1904 Yeats turns explicitly to drama. In 'The Emotion of Multitude' (1903) Yeats explores how drama may accommodate lyric, symbol and vision. What Yeats means by the term 'emotion of multitude' is best captured in his description of *King Lear* as 'less the history of one man and his sorrows than a history of a whole evil time' (*E&I*, p. 214). Yeats views his hero in terms of his context and he pursues that context in 'emotion of multitude', a reverberation that carries us beyond the particular and incidental to the universal and shared.

The essay 'Play, Player and Scene', written shortly after Yeats's first version of *On Baile's Strand*, shows Yeats accommodating the heroic to dramatic format. Yeats grasps the need for a new form of presentation and realises the incompatibility of the heroic with naturalism. His starting-point is a production of Ibsen's *Ghosts*, seen on a small stage. But the naturalistic techniques of the play result in a strange transformation of that small stage. Instead it becomes enormous, an abyss. The actors rather than expressing a close imitation of reality are 'little whimpering puppets': 'Why did they not speak out with louder voices or move with freer gestures? What was it that weighed upon their souls perpetually? Certainly they were all in prison . . . ' (*E*, p. 168). Yeats cannot accept diminishment or imprisonment. His heroes may be weighed down by an anti-heroic world, but they are never anti-heroes. A curious situation develops as Yeats explores anti-naturalistic techniques. By making his players move as puppets, Yeats expresses the full freedom of life where naturalism relying on the imitation of natural gesture and conversation reduces art to a whimpering. But the heroic is exceptional and stands out from the everyday world which Yeats sees as the landscape of naturalistic drama:

> Art delights in the exception, for it delights in the soul expressing itself according to its own laws and arranging the world about it in its own pattern. . . . But the average man is average, because he has not attained to freedom. Habit, routine, fear of public opinion, fear of punishment . . . a myriad things that are 'something other than human life', something less than the flame, work their will upon his soul and trundle his body here and there.   (Ibid.)

A negative definition of the heroic or exceptional man is provided here. This is characteristic of Yeats and allows him to define not only the hero, but also what is opposed to him. The hero emerges as artificer in the sense that he determines his own world and is not moved or swayed by public opinion. He is decidedly not a puppet, but a free man and a visionary. The surface imitation of reality, the average man as protagonist – these things miss the point:

> After all, is not the greatest play, not the play that gives us the greatest sense of an external reality, but the play in which there is the greatest abundance of life itself, of the reality that is in our own minds.   (p. 167)

But this abundant reality undergoes a strange transformation in the tragic process as it embraces death:

The arts are at their greatest when they seek for a life growing always more scornful of everything that is not itself and passing into its own fullness, as it were, ever more completely, as all that is created out of the passing mode of society slips from it; and attaining that fullness, perfectly it may be – and from this is tragic joy and the perfectness of tragedy – when the world itself has slipped away in death.   (pp. 169–70)

The hero does not pass away, but the world passes from him. Yet in the process richness and fullness become their opposite. This element of the tragic process is central to Yeats's treatment of Cuchulain, whose extravagant bravado is continually pitted against and transformed by the waves of a haunted sea.

Relating this process of discovery to technique[26] on the stage, Yeats singles out the three components of the essay's title. The play, that is the words, are first in importance. The actor must 'get away, except in trivial passages, from the methods of conversation' (p. 172). The attention of the audience is to be fixed by a language and an articulation unmarred 'by any irrelevant or obtrusive gesture' (ibid.). Then the player too must tune his movements to a slow deliberate rhythm. The actors should appear as 'paintings on a frieze' (pp. 176–7). Finally the landscape or scene is defined. Yeats banishes naturalism: 'the moment an actor stands near to your mountain, or your forest, one will perceive that he is standing against a flat surface. Illusion, therefore, is impossible, and should not be attempted. One should be content to suggest a scene . . .'(p. 178). Yeats wants a scenic art that 'will give the imagination liberty', for 'the scene should never be complete of itself, should never mean anything to the imagination until the actor is in front of it' (p. 179). Again Yeats is concerned with discovery. The landscape is created in the imagination.

On Baile's Strand (*CPl*, pp. 247–78) reflects this search for an appropriate method of presentation for the heroic and exceptional. The stage directions introduce us to a dominantly naturalistic setting with two elements at war with this naturalism: through a door at the back we see '*misty light as of sea mist*'; the Fool and Blind Man are made '*grotesque and extravagant by masks*'. These two elements are vital to the play. The sea dominates, is in fact one of the protagonists and is allied to the Shape-Changers, witches and deceiving sirens who haunt Cuchulain. The Fool and Blind Man reflect Yeats's concern with 'emotion of multitude', as grotesque shadows of the central conflict. They explain and interpret the plot and they mimic, in parodic form, the battle between Cuchulain and Conchubar. They reflect also the lesser world which vanquishes the hero. Deformed, cunning, self-seeking and idiotic, they are the intermediary audience before whom Cuchulain's drama is played. They frame the actions of the play, introducing and concluding its themes.

The parallel between the Fool and Cuchulain and the Blind Man and Conchubar is established by their relationship. The Fool provides food for the Blind Man but 'can go out and run races with the witches at the edge of the waves and get an appetite'. The Fool, however, is tormented by more than the cunning of his mentor: 'There are some that follow me. Boann herself out of the river and Fand out of the deep sea. Witches they are, and they come by in the wind, and they cry, "Give us a kiss, Fool, give us a kiss" . . . .' The Blind Man's relationship to Conchubar, underlined by his manipulation of the Fool, is established when he sits in Conchubar's chair and acts out for the Fool the coming subjection of hero to High King. 'Cuchulain could do anything he liked', 'But he ran too wild'. Finally the Fool and Blind Man are prosaic. The heroes and kings at the centre of the play are separated and distinguished by their high style of language. In this way Cuchulain is presented to us through the eyes of his inferior. This method is typical of Yeats. Particularly in the dance plays we have to lift layer after layer of association and suggestion to come directly to the hero himself. He is thus presented indirectly and in contrast to those who surround and precede him. He is different, isolated.

But Cuchulain is allowed more direct comment and self-definition in this play than in any other of Yeats's plays. This is largely achieved through contrast with Conchubar. Against Conchubar's charges of irresponsibility, Cuchulain defines the heroic code of behaviour, based as it is on freedom:

> Must I, that held you on the throne when all
> Had pulled you from it, swear obedience
> As if I were some cattle-raising king?

Conchubar constantly provokes Cuchulain into such definition.

The hero sees his legacy in terms of fame and glory. Rather than a child, mere 'pallid ghost', he would 'leave names upon the harp' and he declares 'I would leave / My house and name to none that would not face / Even myself in battle.' This suggests his sense of a diminishing race as well as unconscious irony. Conchubar's taunts, which also have an ironic and threatening undertone, illustrate the excessive nature of the heroic:

> You should have overtaken on the hills
> Some daughter of the air, or on the shore
> A daughter of the Country-under-Wave.

Cuchulain's definition of love underlines this tendency towards excess. That Aoife's love should have turned to hatred is not surprising. Emotions experienced to their full extent turn into their opposites. Lovers are opponents, kindling each other into flame, pursuing each other remorselessly:

> I never have known love but as a kiss
> In the mid-battle, and a difficult truce
> Of oil and water, candles and dark night,
> Hillside and hollow, the hot-footed sun
> And the cold, sliding, slippery-footed moon . . . .[27]

At Cuchulain's final submission to Conchubar his sense of identity and self-definition reaches a climax which is also a bitter acknowledgement of diminishment, betrayal of the heroic code and decay:

> It's time the years put water in my blood
> And drowned the wildness of it, for all's changed,
> But that unchanged. – I'll take what oath you will:
> The moon, the sun, the water, light, or air,
> I do not care how binding.

Cuchulain's reckless 'I do not care how binding' establishes that his destiny is also partly chosen.

At this point the play is interrupted by another anti-naturalistic device. A chorus of women sing to ward off the Shape-Changers. But, instead of retiring to banishment, these now grow in power. For the first time our attention is fully focused on the sea. The Fool's early references, Conchubar's taunts and the presence of the sea all this time in the background build up to a climax with the women's song, while Aoife's love turning to hate is clearly related to the figures of the Shape-Changers. L. E. Nathan in *The Tragic Drama of W. B. Yeats* sums up the significance of this chorus:

> It is, in fact, these powers, female in their attractiveness and shape-changing, that Cuchulain, as a Yeatsian hero, has always pursued, through love which turns to hate and through strength to conquer which turns to self-injury. The end of his quest is the severing of his connection with all human life and a grief which finds only the sea its fit object. Like heroic love, heroic hatred is beyond human objects and touched with witchcraft. The musicians' description of these superhuman and destructive passions of love and hate provides some ground for the excessiveness of Cuchulain's final fury, which without some explanation might seem obscure. The musicians' song makes credible acts that in their frenzy transcend the range of normal human feeling and perception.[28]

The song has an irony in that it is women who sing it, but their song is made

> Against the will of women at its wildest
> In the Shape-Changers that run upon the wind.

In this song the wild of will are conceived in terms of wave, mist and wind. They are unattainable and tormenting muses:

> The women none can kiss and thrive,
> For they are but whirling wind . . . .
> They would make a prince decay
> With light images of clay
> Planted in the running wave . . . .

Their enchantments are cruel and destructive. Their cruelty,

> That he follow with desire
> Bodies that can never tire

is less terrible than their kindness. For the man whom these women have favoured is 'thrice forlorn':

> Emptied, ruined, wracked and lost,
> That they follow, for at most
> They will give him kiss for kiss
> While they murmur, 'After this
> Hatred may be sweet to the taste.'

The effect of this song is to introduce a wider dimension than that of the conflict between the political Conchubar with his limiting compromise, and the foolhardy hero. These forces are beyond control or reason, and Conchubar's words as he seals the oath, 'I give my wisdom, and I take your strength', belong to an ordered world which ignores and is undermined by the powers of the sea. Cuchulain's battle is internal. He is as much at war with himself as with Conchubar.

The contest with his unknown son is a part of this. Father and son are kin in their heroic behaviour. The son defines himself by heroic criteria: 'I will give no other proof than the hawk gives / That it's no sparrow!' Cuchulain recognises his kinship:

> This fighting's welcome.
> The High King there has promised me his wisdom;
> But the hawk's sleepy till its well-beloved
> Cries out amid the acorns, or it has seen
> Its enemy like a speck upon the sun.
> What's wisdom to the hawk, when that clear eye
> Is burning nearer up in the high air?

He takes the boy for ally, 'Because you have a hot heart and a cold eye'. Indeed, he unwittingly acknowledges his son's true identity:

> Boy, I would meet them all in arms
> If I'd a son like you. He would avenge me
> When I have withstood for the last time the men
> Whose fathers, brothers, sons and friends I have killed . . . .

Cuchulain is trapped by two loyalties – to his heroic identity and to his oath with Conchubar – but beneath lies the web woven by the Shape-Changers. Conchubar warns, 'Some witch of the air has troubled Cuchulain's mind', 'A witch of the air / Can make a leaf confound us with memories'. The hero is doubly confounded, for Conchubar, though opposed to the irrational forces of the sea, nevertheless manipulates Cuchulain's response to them, in this way ensuring that Aoife's revenge succeeds. Throughout Cuchulain is drawn to his final confrontation with the sea. A threefold deception is cast on him by Aoife, Conchubar and the Shape-Changers, to whom he succumbs – 'Yes, witchcraft! witchcraft! Witches of the air!' – and love of his unknown son turns to hatred.

There is no further direct representation of the conflict. The Fool and Blind Man return to mimic the relationship between Cuchulain and Conchubar. The Blind Man has tricked the Fool. 'You take care of me?' he cries, 'You stay safe, and send me into every kind of danger.' Although Cuchulain returns to the stage, his reactions are almost entirely related to us by this grotesque pair. When Cuchulain learns what he has done, it is they who tell us this: 'Somebody is trembling, Fool! The bench is shaking', says the Blind Man. The Fool responds, 'It is Cuchulain who is trembling. It is Cuchulain who is shaking the bench.' The Blind Man completes the tale: 'It is his own son he has slain.' Cuchulain, baffled and perplexed, lashes out against both the supernatural world and the politic world of Conchubar. He is searching for a tangible enemy against which to pit a grief and an anger which can have no limit. Yet this destiny is partly chosen, since he has freely made his oath. His final rage, related to us by the Fool, is appropriate to the relentless tide of choice, deception and consequence. But it shows the hero in a bizarre light. His simple code, his hawklike freedom bound by oath, can find no answer to complexity but gesture. He is a man fighting the waves, a man shouting in the dark: 'He has killed kings and giants, but the waves have mastered him, the waves have mastered him!' To Blind Man and Fool the great gesture is subsidiary if useful. The house is empty, but the ovens are full.

Yeats's attempts to break out of a naturalistic convention in this play are not wholly successful. But an exploration of Yeats's own dissatisfactions with the play help to focus attention on the version of the heroic which Yeats is struggling to evoke in the figure of Cuchulain and the direction he will follow from this point onwards. Denis Donoghue remarks, 'Regardless of the official endorsement of personality, the play is based upon contrasts of character, particularly [of] Cuchulain and Conchubar.'[29] In a letter to Frank Fay, Yeats comments on the apparent intractability of dramatic form: 'epic and folk-literature can ignore time as drama does not – Helen never ages, Cuchulain never ages' (*L*, p. 424). But in drama he does. He must, argues Yeats, be old enough to have a grown son. In addition this concern with linear time brings in elements of motivation and character. These tend to make Cuchulain particular rather than universal or archetypal. Conchubar's discussion of the motives for Cuchulain's childlessness, and his suggestions that Cuchulain secretly yearns for a son, contradict the image that Yeats would present of the hero:

> The touch of something hard, repellent yet alluring, self-assertive yet self-immolating, is not all but it must be there. He is the fool – wandering passive, houseless and almost loveless. Conchubar is reason that is blind because it can only reason because it is cold. Are they not the hot sun and the cold moon? (*L*, p. 425)

Later, in a note on the Noh theatre, Yeats remarks on the inability of linear time to define landscape, to reveal its significance:

> I could lay the scene of a play on Baile's strand, but I found no pause in the hurried action for descriptions of strand or sea . . . . But in the *Nishikigi* the tale of the lovers would lose its pathos if we did not see the forgotten tomb where the 'hiding fox' lives . . . . (*E&I*, p. 233)

Yeats is searching for a mode of presenting mythic truth.

In three essays between 1907 and 1910 Yeats explores and clarifies the transformation which occurs in the tragic moment, the moment in which the hero achieves vision and is transformed in the face of death. In 'Poetry and Tradition' Yeats creates the poet as hero and aristocrat, free, abundant, in the circle of self-delight, separated from chaos and self-interest. This is Cuchulain as the hawk, his blood undiluted. But Yeats's essay ends with a slipping-away from abundance into triumphant penury: 'Shakespeare's persons, when the last darkness has gathered about them, speak out of an ecstacy that is one-half the self-surrender of sorrow, and one-half the last playing and mockery of the victorious sword before the defeated world' (*E&I*, p. 254).

In 'The Tragic Theatre' and in 'Synge and the Ireland of his Times' Synge provides Yeats with a central focus for his definition of tragic joy. In 'The Tragic Theatre' of 1910 Yeats's whole attention is focused on this paradoxical moment. The essay begins with Synge's *Deirdre of the Sorrows*. Synge's Deirdre approaches death with a wealth of extravagant language and image:

> because of me there will be weasels and wild cats crying on a lonely wall where there were Queens and armies and red gold, the way there will be a story told of a ruined city and a raving king and a woman will be young forever . . . . I have put away sorrow like a shoe that is worn out and muddy, for it is I have had a life that will be envied by great companies. . . . It's a pitiful thing, Conchubar, you have done this night in Emain, yet a thing will be a joy and triumph to the ends of life and time.[30]

In Yeats's response we find ourselves in an area the opposite of extravagance:

> we knew that the player had become if but for a moment the creature of that noble mind which had gathered its art in waste islands and we too were carried beyond time and persons to where passion, living through its thousand purgatorial years, as in the wink of an eye, becomes wisdom; and it was as though we too had touched and seen a disembodied thing.   (*E&I*, p. 239)

Thus for Yeats the abundance of life becomes 'disembodied'. This moment is a revelation to him. Tragedy he sees is the 'art of the flood' (p. 242), breaking down the dykes between man and man. The hero is isolated from ordinary life. Hamlet is shown 'broken away from life by the passionate hesitations of his reverie' (ibid.). Tragedy uses devices to lessen character. It all but banishes the everyday world and fills the empty places with 'rhythm, balance, pattern, images that remind us of vast passions, the vagueness of past times, all the chimeras that haunt the edge of trance' (p. 243). The face of tragedy is empty, potential, waiting 'the supreme crisis' (p. 244). With this trance-like and disembodied state we find ourselves in a new region and at this climax of tragedy, 'there comes upon one the strange sensation as though the hair of one's head stood up' (p. 243).

In 'Synge and the Ireland of his Times' Yeats tells us that Synge 'loves all that has edge, all that is salt in the mouth, all that is rough to the hand, all that heightens the emotions by contest, all that stings into life the sense of tragedy' (*E&I*, pp. 326–7).[31] In this description Yeats is close to Synge, to the vivid abundance of life in his plays, but already he is transforming Synge into an ascetic, astringent refinement of personality. The wealth of Synge's created world is vanishing away. Synge is becoming a Nietzschean hero. His 'creative joy' contains 'an acceptance of what life brings, because we have understood the beauty of what it brings, or a hatred of death for what it takes away' (p. 322). This arouses 'an energy so noble, so powerful, that we laugh aloud and mock, in the terror or the sweetness of our exaltation, at death and oblivion' (ibid.). Yeats now defines art as 'the disengaging of a soul from place and history, its suspension in a beautiful or terrible light, to await the Judge-ment' (p. 339). Art, which he had earlier defined as a spirit quickening every emotion and passion in man, reaches its final crisis in death, in the light of a judgement day. Such art, as Yeats had earlier remarked of Hyde's collection of folktales, adds not to mere accumulation of factual knowledge but to our being. Synge belongs with Shakespeare, Dante and Goethe. He recreates man 'not through the eyes or in history, or even in the future, but . . . in the depths of the mind, and in all art like his . . . may lie the roots of far-branching events' (p. 341).

This call to the depths of the mind will become increasingly familiar to us in Yeats's dance plays. Yeats's response to the extraordinary moment of tragic joy focuses as much on the response of the audience as on the central figure. Drama is to be a re-creation in the imagination. The hero is to be recognised within ourselves in 'waste islands', beyond 'a thousand purga-torial years'. Synge's 'waste islands' off the western seaboard become the landscape for Yeats's drama, the physical embodi-ment of a state which is disembodied and ghostly. The implica-tions for Cuchulain, here, are that he becomes a mask through which the audience may discover for themselves the process of tragic recognition and joy.

In defining Yeats's response to Cuchulain it will be helpful here to look briefly at two other plays of this decade. In *The King's Threshold* (1904) and in *Deirdre* (1907) Yeats is concerned with heroic integrity and tragic consequence. But Yeats's treatment of the heroic is very different in these plays from his treatment of Cuchulain. Both Seanchan and Deirdre are articulate. Seanchan is never baffled or bewildered. There is no interior conflict and little complexity in *The King's Threshold* (*CPL*, pp. 107–43). Seanchan stands on principle. Unlike Cuchulain's, his defeat is clearly a victory. He is not trapped, but superior to the forces of politics. He clearly diagnoses the condition of the world, 'the white of leprosy / And the contagion that afflicts mankind'. He speaks to a future when the heroic may again triumph. He can laugh in the face of defeat and voice his paradoxical victory:

> I need no help.
> He needs no help that joy has lifted up
> Like some miraculous beast out of Ezekiel.
> The man that dies has the chief part in the story . . . .

Deirdre (*CPl*, pp. 171–203) is a far more complex exploration of the heroic, but again, unlike Cuchulain, Deirdre is at all times coherent and articulate. As Rajan suggests in his interesting study of the play, Deirdre understands the nature of tragedy's characteristic gesture, death.[32] But to achieve this end she has to employ cunning and deceit. She is able to outwit the lesser and anti-heroic world by using its tricks. The world is not only hostile to tragedy and its gestures, but, as we have seen in *On Baile's Strand*, unimpressed by it, treating it as matter for mockery. Deirdre cannot change this world, but she can free herself from it, write her own destiny. As Rajan points out, the danger facing Deirdre is not death, but the failure to achieve a heroic death. Rajan sees Yeats as moving away from the conventional portrayal of the heroic, and *Deirdre*, he argues, is 'almost a luxury, an ornate digression from the stern line of Yeats's advance'.[33] The play reveals what tragedy may have to abandon: '"Everything sublunary must change", including the assumptions of tragedy itself . . . . If creative defiance is to be achieved, it must be achieved within that self-born mockery which arises from the fact of being man . . . .'[34] Whether or not Yeats does move so unequivocably from the gesture of heroic death is questionable, and the archaic nature of the gesture is brought sharply into contemporary focus by the events of 1916. But Deirdre, facing an increasingly hostile environment, greatly increases the subtlety of the tragic encounter.

Another element in the play which needs to be mentioned is its technique. Although the play is given a naturalistic setting, this is used symbolically to define the nature of the tragic conflict. The cottage interior gains significance because it is a trap. The sea and wilderness outside are contrasted with the limiting of the action within four walls:

> King, she is dead; but lay no hand upon her.
> What's this but empty cage and tangled wire,
> Now that the bird's gone?

Yeats uses the chorus in an original way. The singing women control the action of the play and tell its story. They instruct us. But it is Deirdre who instructs them, giving them a bracelet, 'To show that you have Deirdre's story right'. Where Cuchulain is content to recognise that 'you and I leave names upon the harp', Deirdre writes her own song:

O, singing women, set it down in a book,
That love is all we need, even though it is
But the last drops we gather up like this;
And though the drops are all we have known of life,
For we have been most friendless – praise us for it,
And praise the double sunset, for naught's lacking
But a good end to the long, cloudy day.

One might also note that at the end of the play the musicians light fleetingly, almost accidentally, on what becomes Yeats's characteristic landscape for tragedy:

FIRST MUSICIAN.   They are gone, they are gone.
SECOND MUSICIAN.   Whispering were enough.
FIRST MUSICIAN.   Into the secret wilderness of their love.
SECOND MUSICIAN.   A high, grey cairn. What more is to be said?

What is it that so differentiates Cuchulain from either of these two heroic figures, Seanchan and Deirdre? On a rather mundane level it is, perhaps, the fact that each of these plays is complete in itself, ending with the gesture of death. With Cuchulain we are dealing with a cycle of plays. Yet each of Cuchulain's encounters is with a potential death. The difference, I feel, lies in the fact that tragic conflict in Cuchulain is both internal and external. Deirdre may use the weapons of a hostile world to achieve her end, but she is not at war with herself.[35] With Cuchulain, too, there is a sense of the strange or eerie in which brave deeds are stripped away. Neither in *On Baile's Strand* nor in the dance plays to follow is the hero's culminating gesture in any way close to our ordinary conceptions of joy.

I conclude this chapter with a brief discussion of *The Green Helmet* (*CPl*, pp. 223–43). This play is something of a curiosity in Yeats's Cuchulain cycle, a singular example as it is of a genre Yeats titles 'Heroic farce'.[36] Helen Vendler describes this play as 'a fairly trivial comment on the literary and political contentiousness which prevents the Irish from attaining effective unity'.[37] I must confess that this is not an interpretation which I find altogether sufficient, but I am inclined to agree that the play is 'fairly trivial'. It does however outline the nature of the heroic in a positive manner, and its stress on behaviour is characteristic of Yeats's later insistence on the aristocratic, noble and magnanimous.

In this play Yeats abandons naturalism in a thoroughly agressive manner. The house is orange, the sea a vivid green; the indigenous inhabitants are all dressed in green, while the Black Men have eyes which '*should look green from the reflected light of the sea*'. The Red Man is obviously dressed in red, while he wears a green, horned helmet and '*The effect is intentionally violent and startling.*' This anti-naturalistic effect is augmented by the use of couplets throughout. The aggressive stridency of the techniques is suited also to the satirical element of the play, its presentation of a house in disorder.

Throughout the play Cuchulain's behaviour is in contrast to that of every other character. He alone stands up to the monster. At each quarrel for precedence Cuchulain adopts a magnanimous stance. He is willing to share the helmet. When the wives quarrel he is generous. The Red Man's wager is in jest, and he comes to choose the true champion, Cuchulain, because of his recklessness and laughter, 'The hand that loves to scatter; the life like a gambler's throw'. He prophesies the coming decay:

> And these things I make prosper, till a day comes that I
>   know,
> When heart and mind shall darken that the weak may
>   end the strong,
> And the long-remembering harpers have matter for their
>   song.

But Emer's song, breaking away from the rigid couplet, is as fitting a tribute to the strength of the heroic temperament. Emer can find no particular deed to cause her elation:

> Nothing that he has done;
> His mind that is fire,
> His body that is sun,
> Have set my head higher
> Than all the world's wives.

The hero's gift is himself:

> Himself on the wind
> Is the gift that he gives . . . .

He is almost life itself in its fullest strength. He is sun and fire, as Emer is moon and steel. She is all that sets off and complements the hero.

It will be helpful, when exploring Cuchulain in the context of the Japanese Noh, to remember this wholly triumphant evocation of the heroic, despite its triviality, in much of this play. The dance plays with their powerful landscapes tend to obscure the heroic character in their midst, and, as Yeats discovers new territory and his hero new vision, he may be seen as leaving behind a certain vitality. Nothing will show this more clearly than a comparison of the effect of a line from *The Great Helmet* and a similar line in the later *At the Hawk's Well*. In the fullness of his strength Cuchulain here defines himself: 'I am Sualtim's son, Cuchulain – What do you laugh in my face?' We shall have to compare this with Cuchulain's self-definition in the later play: 'He comes! Cuchulain, son of Sualtim, comes!' (*CPl*, p. 218).

2 The Landscape of Tragedy: Three Dance Plays

In the last chapter, I explored Yeats's search for a new method of dramatic presentation. In this search, I suggested, Yeats concentrates on vision, leading his hero towards revelation. Cuchulain moves from an abundance of life and gesture into a place of emptiness, a suspension in the light of a judgement day, a waste land. Such transformation is achieved in the tragic moment, when the everyday world is left behind. This chapter explores three plays, *At the Hawk's Well* (1917), *The Only Jealousy of Emer* (1919) and *The Dreaming of the Bones* (1919). Heavily influenced by the Japanese Noh theatre, these plays show Yeats's discovery of a form which removes all reference to a naturalistic imitation of the world. The problems Yeats had encountered with character, linear time and place are now resolved. Yeats is able to concentrate on the moment of tragic recognition, on the tragic encounter between the hero and his opposite. But in this development, it may be argued, Yeats's hero loses stature, power and, significantly, accessibility to the audience. The new structure of presentation, which appeals to the 'mind's eye' of the audience, may be seen as counter-productive.

Opinion on Yeats's dance plays veers between praise for the appropriate form and criticism of it as obscure and too far removed from ordinary human experience. L. E. Nathan describes Yeats as rejecting both the new naturalistic and the traditional face of drama. Even Shakespeare is not an altogether satisfactory model. Yeats, Nathan argues, 'regarded such drama as essentially concerned with the working out of man's fate in the natural world':[1] 'the supernatural, even in *Macbeth*, hardly suggests the war of orders that is central to Yeats's conception of reality'.² Nathan defines this war as between living and dead, nature and spirit. Man is faced with 'a heroic inner struggle':

> for he participates through his passions in the spiritual or immortal but is after all a creature bound by his natural limits. The war forces on him a choice between two mutually antagonistic worlds, two ways of life, two sets of values. He cannot have both; by choosing one he falls victim to the other. Thus man was, for Yeats, the centre of cosmic tension.³

In order to present this war Yeats had to create a new form, since none of the available modes of presentation was adequate. Barton Friedman, in his study of Yeats's drama *Adventures in the Deeps of the Mind*, centres on the isolation of the tragic moment, the idea of suspension in the light of a judgement day. He argues that Yeats, in the Cuchulain cycle, is intent on freeing man from 'the nightmare of history'.⁴ Yeats replaces this with an appeal to man's innermost psyche and drama becomes 'a vehicle for attuning him to this innermost aspect of himself'.⁵ In other words, as Yeats suggests in the essay 'Play, Player and Scene', art should reflect the reality of our minds, rather than the superficial external world. For Yeats, Friedman argues, the play evokes 'a moment set apart': 'Figures in Yeatsian drama are not characters . . . but aspects of a character: personified ideas, emotions, impulses insulated from all other ideas, emotions, impulses.'⁶

Friedman argues that Yeats's tragic heroes are single-minded and obsessive. The hero 'becomes what he enacts, which is to say, he becomes what Yeats calls a Daimon'.⁷ For this reason Friedman sees Yeats as successful in the new mode of presentation we meet in *At the Hawk's Well*: 'Its setting is the mind of the playwright gestating the play, its triumph the attainment of a method for inducing the audience to live that process: to become for the dramatic moment artists shaping an artifact.'⁸

Other critics, however, are less than happy with this new direction. Richard Taylor in *Irish Myth and the Japanese Nō* comments on the contemporary failure of the reception of the dance plays. He sees Yeats as being both too out-of-date and too *avant-garde*:

> The trouble with Yeats's dance plays was that in addition to an almost obsolete heroic apparatus and an altogether

outdated occultism, his production method was highly styl-
ized and aggressively anti-illusionist. However well-suited to
his subject-matter and theatrical aims, the non-realistic and
expressive staging of the dance dramas was not yet acceptable
to the theatre-going public and proved to be another
stumbling-block to the reception of his work.[9]

The plays remain inaccessible to some critics. Helen Vendler
sees Yeats's plays as valuable only in so far as they provide a
poetics: 'My concern, however, is not with Yeats as a playwright –
I think his gifts in the purely theatrical direction were limited,
to say the least.'[10] Their failure as plays is related to their lack of
connection with recognisable human experience. She quotes
from I. A. Richards to sum up her response:

> After a drawn battle with the drama, Mr. Yeats made a
> violent repudiation, not merely of current civilisation but of
> life itself, in favour of a supernatural world. . . . Now he turns
> to a world of symbolic phantasmagoria about which he is
> desperately uncertain. He is uncertain because he had
> adopted as a technique of inspiration the use of trance, of
> dissociated phases of consciousness, and the revelations given
> in these dissociated states are insufficiently connected with
> normal experience.[11]

Where Friedman argues that such dissociated states are con-
nected with Yeats's attempts to unite man with his psyche, and
that in *At the Hawk's Well* the audience participates in the
process, Vendler and Richards feel that he fails. The audience is
not involved. The difference between these two views is largely
the subjective response of the audience. I feel that Friedman is
correct in his definition of the aims of Yeats's theatre. And
technically the device of the chorus in the dance plays, with their
calling on the eye of the mind, must be seen as successful. But
the subjective response of the audience is important if Yeats is to
succeed in his aim of evoking 'the supreme moment of tragic art'
(*E&I*, p. 238). We shall have to examine the question of response in relation to each of the dance plays.
    My argument is that Yeats, in these plays, is not attempting to
write tragedies. He is writing about tragedy, exploring elements
of the tragic situation. His work as a whole may present what

Nathan describes as man at the centre of cosmic tension, but the plays concentrate on a moment, the moment of tragic joy. Yeats, I feel, is intent on the cathartic moment, on a redefinition of Aristotle's pity and fear with his response of terror and delight. Yeats's answer to charges of dissociation from human experience, to remoteness, the problem of conveying the intangible emotional transformation of the tragic moment, is expressed in the play's construction of a landscape. The waste land which Yeats's dance plays reveal is both an emotional state and a place, a landscape which we inhabit for the play's duration.

Before exploring the plays, we should look at Yeats's response to the Japanese Noh theatre.[12] The Noh theatre provides Yeats with a convention in which to crystallise the views we have seen developing. In his Introduction to *Certain Noble Plays of Japan*, Yeats restates many of his theories, but he can now organise them in a more coherent and practicable fashion. He begins by relating *At the Hawk's Well* to the impact made on his imagination by a Japanese dancer:

> My play is made possible by a Japanese dancer whom I have seen dance in a studio and in a drawing-room and on a very small stage. . . . In the studio and in the drawing-room alone, where the lighting was the light we are most accustomed to, did I see him as the tragic image that has stirred my imagination. There, where no studied lighting, no stage-picture made an artificial world, he was able, as he rose from the floor, where he had been sitting cross-legged, or as he threw out an arm, to recede from us into some more powerful life. Because that separation was achieved by human means alone, he receded but to inhabit as it were the deeps of the mind. One realised anew, at every separating strangeness, that the measure of all arts' greatness can be but in their intimacy.   (*E&I*, p. 224)

Just as Yeats saw Synge's art emerge from 'the deeps of the mind' rather than from external reality, Yeats now sees that drama takes place in the mind or imagination of the spectator. Now he can see a way of achieving this vision. By abandoning every artifice of theatre, by relying solely on movement and gesture, the dancer reaches into the mind; by distancing himself he achieves intimacy. Where in 'The Tragic Theatre' Yeats had recognised the need for 'rhythm, balance, pattern' (p. 243), he now sees all art as deliberate, even aristocratic:

All imaginative art remains at a distance and this distance, once chosen, must be firmly held against a pushing world. Verse, ritual, music, and dance in association with action require that gesture, costume, facial expression, stage arrangement must help in keeping the door.   (p. 224)

Where before Yeats had used mask to make the Fool and Blind Man grotesque, he now uses mask as a technique for distancing us from circumstantial reality: 'A mask never seems but a dirty face, and no matter how close you go is yet a work of art; nor shall we lose by stilling the movement of the features, for deep feeling is expressed by a movement of the whole body'(p. 226). Just as the writer is not to seek his art from the mirror, not merely to reflect the everyday, but to create, to be conscious, the actor in a mask is no longer imitating the gestures of one particular man.

Allied to mask, a style of movement provides Yeats with another distancing-technique. Yeats finds a clear correspondence between the stylised movement of the Noh players and the aim of their theatre:

The players wear masks and found their movements upon those of puppets. . . . A swift or a slow movement and a long or a short stillness, and then another movement. They sing as much as they speak, and [the chorus] . . . never becomes . . . a part of the action. At the climax, instead of the disordered passion of nature, there is a dance, a series of positions and movements which may represent a battle, or a marriage, or the pain of a ghost . . . .   (p. 230)

It is the distance which Yeats applauds, the keeping of a door against the pushing world of everyday reality. The dance at the end represents an action. It does not imitate one. Movements are tense. The body is poised for action, refusing to be overwhelmed, disordered or fragmented. The Noh plays do not seek to re-create man as he walks this way and that, but aim to reveal what is essential:

The interest is not in the human form but in the rhythm to which it moves, and the triumph of their art is to express the rhythm in its intensity. There are few swaying movements of

arms or body . . . . They move from the hip . . . and seem to associate with every gesture or pose some definite thought.
(p. 231)

Their actions are always definite, rehearsed and ceremonious.

Finally, the Noh provides Yeats with a dramatic form in which language can predominate. Words are linked to action through the importance of place. In Noh drama the imagined scene of the action is always invested with awe. The place with its history or mythology becomes inseparable from the story acted within it. This will become true of Yeats's dance plays. His stunted trees and rocky hill-tops become the central image for barren passion, timeless experience, for the characteristic sense of defeat and its underlying bitterness. The Noh theatre shows Yeats how to make use of a chorus in conjunction with an intermediary figure to define the landscape: 'it pleases them to begin so many plays by a traveller asking his way with many questions, a convention agreeable to me' (p. 232). In the dance plays Yeats uses the chorus to define place, and in *The Dreaming of the Bones*, the closest of all in structure to the Noh, he uses the intermediary figure and the process of a journey. Yeats's ideas on tragedy and on an anti-naturalistic technique were born independently of the Noh, as we have seen. Its main significance is as a model. Yeats does, however, differ significantly from the aims of the Noh in that he represents failure and defeat, where the Noh plays reveal order and reconciliation.

The essay 'Anima Hominis' (1917) enlightens aspects of Yeats's drama as well as being the point of departure for *A Vision*. If the Noh theatre illustrates new technical possibilities, Yeats's theories on the tragic encounter in this essay clarify and expand the understanding of the heroic we explored in the last chapter: the meeting of opposites typified by Cuchulain's relationship with the Sidhe, the transformation of abundance to penury and the revelation of an inner or essential reality. The tragic encounter, with its paradoxical meeting between elation and desolation, when man becomes or meets his Daimon, finds a central image in the mask. We have to distinguish two ways in which Yeats uses the term: the anti-naturalistic device, and the idea of a mask as something which enables us to glimpse 'a disembodied thing', 'the tragic image', the other world. Through the mask two worlds are brought face to face. A timeless or elemental world is revealed and allowed to take shape in the mind or imagination, once surface or superficial reality is dismissed.

The mask as defined in 'Anima Hominis' allows us to meet what Yeats terms the 'anti-self'. Yeats sees this anti-self in the life and work of all great artists and creators. Their art is born out of a struggle between opposing aspects of their natures: 'I comprehend, if I know the lineaments of his life, that the work is the man's flight from his entire horoscope, his blind struggle in the net-work of the stars' (*M*, p. 328). Yeats gives this anti-self the name of Daimon. He invents a story which pictures the meeting of these opposites. Some legendary hero, he suggests, may have found 'hanging upon some oak . . . an ancient mask' (p. 335). By putting up this mask to his face, the hero sees, through strange eyes, a stranger's world: 'he knew another's breath came and went within his breath upon the carven lips, and that his eyes were upon the instant fixed upon a visionary world' (ibid.). This moment of revelation is achieved by a transformation of opposites. The Daimon or anti-self is mysterious where the self is obvious. But they are also antagonistic, each seeking to devour the other:

> the Daimon comes not as like to like but seeking its own opposite, for man and Daimon feed the hunger in one another's hearts. Because the ghost is simple, the man heterogeneous and confused, they are but knit together when the man has found a mask whose lineaments permit the expression of all the man most lacks, and it may be dreads, and of that only. (Ibid.)

In order to see this visionary world, man must adopt a heroic and tragic role, must face all that threatens him. The mask in this sense is almost a religious emblem.

It is perhaps this sense of knowing another's breath to be breathing within one's own that shapes our joy in the tragic theatre. Images made pure and intense, actions ceremonious and rehearsed, masked faces brings us out of confusion into clarity, through what Yeats calls 'a thousand purgatorial years'. Yeats does provide us with a possible link between mask as a theatrical technique and mask as the quasi-religious image of tragic confrontation. This emerges as part of his war against naturalistic writing, in favour of discovery:

Some years ago I began to realise that our culture, with its doctrine of sincerity and self-realisation, made us gentle and passive, and that the Middle Ages and the Renaissance were right to found theirs upon the imitation of Christ or some classical hero. Saint Francis and Caesar Borgia made themselves overmastering, creative persons by turning from the mirror to meditation upon a mask.   (p. 333)

We shall see how in *The Only Jealousy of Emer*, Yeats makes use of the mask in both these ways.

In my discussion of the dance plays I am most concerned with their structure. A few general critical remarks will illustrate the context in which I intend to work. Denis Donoghue tells us that the chief significance of Yeats's discovery of the Noh was the discovery of 'a form capable of gathering energy within its own movement: conflict is internal and external, no feeling is allowed to escape from the the form'.[13] The form of Noh theatre, then, helps Yeats achieve an adequate objective correlative for the themes of his drama. David Clark paraphrases and interprets Yeats's conception of reality on the stage. The paradox of the dance plays 'is that they are a return to a deeper realism through cleansing away all devices of circumstantial realism'.[14] This 'imitative quality'

> is enhanced by the scene-painting in words which the lack of scenery makes necessary. The action takes place not in a cardboard world, but in the real world, recognised and coloured by the imagination. The objective solidity of place gives a reality to event and a concreteness to speech which simultaneously makes the ghostly action more intangible (by contrast) and more convincing (by having a local habitation). The play is no longer 'made up', happening in a void. The strange action expresses the spirit of an actual place and borrows objectivity from it; the place on the other hand receives value from the expression in action of its history or meaning.[15]

But what or where exactly is this habitation? What is its significance?

Harold Bloom in his discussion of *At the Hawk's Well* remarks, I think correctly, that the most memorable event of the play is its context (or landscape). Cuchulain is the hero, but what remains with the audience are 'the waste lands against which Cuchulain flares'.[16] In an essay of 1914, 'Swedenborg, Mediums and the Desolate Places', Yeats comments on what will become the characteristic landscape of his plays:

> So heaven and hell are built always anew and in hell or in heaven all do what they please and all are surrounded by scenes and circumstances which are the expression of their natures and the creation of their thought. Swedenborg, because he belongs to an eighteenth century not yet touched by the romantic revival, feels horror amid rocky uninhabited places, and so believes that the evil are in such places while the good are amid smooth grass and garden walks and the clear sunlight of Claude Lorraine.   (*E*, p. 37)

For Yeats this 'rocky uninhabited' landscape is immensely powerful. It is neither good nor evil, though it evokes horror. We sense its capacity to daunt and subdue in the opening chorus of *At the Hawks Well* (*CPl*, pp. 207–20):

> I call to the eye of the mind
> A well long choked up and dry
> And boughs long stripped by the wind,
> And I call to the mind's eye
> Pallor of an ivory face,
> Its lofty dissolute air,
> A man climbing up to a place
> The salt sea wind has swept bare.

Yeats's notes on this play remind us of his debts to the Noh theatre. He defends his use of mask:

> what could be more suitable than that Cuchulain, let us say, a half-supernatural legendary person, should show us a face, not made before the looking-glass by some leading player – there too we have many quarrels – but moulded by some distinguished artist. (*VPl*, p. 416)

There is no backdrop imitating the scene: '*The stage is any bare space before a wall against which stands a patterned screen.*' The start of the play is heralded by the folding and unfolding of a black cloth which is figured with the pattern of a hawk. The musicians begin the play with this action. They control its performance. Their opening song creates the scene before us, inviting the audience to build up the scene in the mind's eye, windswept, barren and desolate. The First Musician talks of despair and defeat. He introduces the Old Man:

> What were his life soon done!
> Would he lose by that or win?
> A mother that saw her son
> Doubled over a speckled shin,
> Cross-grained with ninety years,
> Would cry, 'How little worth
> Were all my hopes and fears
> And the hard pain of his birth!'

Mixed with desolation, then, is futility and defeat. The musicians pick up their instruments while the Guardian of the Well takes up her position. Again everything is achieved with the minimum of suggestion. The Guardian lays beside her *'a square blue cloth to represent a well'*. The musicians build up our apprehension of the place, intensifying the atmosphere with restless foreboding. The song is divided between the three musicians so that they answer and reinforce one another. One musician cries,

> The boughs of the hazel shake,
> The sun goes down in the west.

This is taken up by another voice:

> The heart would be always awake,
> The heart would turn to its rest.

The First Musician describes the sun's fall, the leaves choking the well, the listless actions of its guardian. The Second Musician responds, 'I am afraid of this place.' The song becomes a refrain of opposites which will haunt the play.

In her study of the play, Helen Vendler ingeniously assigns the lines of the musicians between Old Man and Cuchulain.[17] The Old Man, she suggests, is a coward and a failure, Cuchulain the hero and beyond futility. In my reading of the play, however, Yeats does not come down so absolutely on one side or the other. The chorus is there primarily to evoke atmosphere and place. This atmosphere is a tension between rest and restlessness, between the world of the Sidhe and the human world. When the Second Musician tells us, 'I am afraid of this place', he is describing not the cowardice of the Old Man, but fear in a sense related to awe and apprehension. And in the final stanzas of the play, which we shall come to shortly, I feel Helen Vendler is wrong in her interpretation of these lines as a reference to the failure of the Old Man. These differences of interpretation lie in the fact of Helen Vendler's concentration on the theme of heroism, so tending to ignore the qualifications to this implied by a landscape which desolates and overwhelms.[18]

As the Guardian takes up her position, the musicians merge into the background, though they accompany the actions of the players with their instruments. For example, when the Old Man enters,

> *He lifts his head at the sound of a drum-tap. He goes towards the front of the stage moving to the taps of the drum. . . . His movements, like those of the other persons of the play, suggest a marionette.*

The musicians interrupt the action at crucial moments. Cuchulain, leaving the well as it is about to fill up, 'has lost what may not be found'. It is the musicians who build up the tension as the Guardian of the Well is possessed and begins to dance:

> O God, protect me
> From a horrible deathless body
> Sliding through the veins of a sudden.

It is the musicians, alone, who see the well as it fills up with water: 'I have heard water plash; it comes, it comes; / Look where it glitters.' In fact the musicians provide the framework of the play, stating and restating its images and evoking its eerie atmosphere. The unfolding and folding of the cloth at the end formally closes the play. The musicians return us to the ordinary world, retreating from the atmosphere of desolation and strife:

> Come to me, human faces
> Familiar memories;
> I have found hateful eyes
> Among the desolate places,
> Unfaltering, unmoistened eyes.

The musicians set against the luring quality of the other world a tension. The play is ambiguous. The closing lines refer not only to the Old Man; Cuchulain cannot escape their ambiguous judgement:

> Folly alone I cherish . . .
> I am content to perish;
> I am but a mouthful of sweet air.
>
> O lamentable shadows,
> Obscurity of strife!
> I choose a pleasant life
> Among indolent meadows;
> Wisdom must live a bitter life.

Is wisdom folly? The musicians leave us undecided:

> Who but an idiot would praise
> Dry stones in a well? . . .
> Who but an idiot would praise
> A withered tree?

The musicians, then, are the means through which Yeats gives the play a unity of image and theme. They distance the players from us; they also control them and bring them to life within our own minds.

Within this framework, what of Cuchulain and the Old Man? I feel that the play's setting tends to dwarf both. The Old Man is an obvious foil to Cuchulain. He is weak, helpless and cowardly. Yeats use him to explain the plot. He is, significantly, seen in the same terms as the landscape. He is as much a figure of desolation as the leafless tree and the dry choked well. He describes the Guardian to Cuchulain, prophesying the action to follow:

> There falls a curse
> On all who have gazed in her unmoistened eyes;
> So get you gone while you have that proud step . . . .

The well of the play's title becomes irrelevant to the action.
Instead it is the woman of the Sidhe, the anti-self, who domi-
nates. The Old Man, hearing the hawk's cry, describes how the
Guardian is possessed by the Sidhe:

> It was her mouth, and yet not she, that cried.
> It was that shadow cried behind her mouth; . . .
> Look at her shivering now, the terrible life
> Is slipping through her veins.

This is the sign that the well will bubble up with water. But
Yeats's real concern in the play is to place Cuchulain in conflict
with the Sidhe. When the Guardian is possessed, she parallels
the position of man in conflict with this other world. As the poet
facing his muse, or as the hero facing his doom, she stands in
relation to her other self as hawk, dancer, and woman of the
Sidhe. The Old Man tells us that she will awake out of her trance
'in ignorance of it all'.

Helen Vendler connects this sleep with the sleep of the Old
Man. It could also be related to Cuchulain's awaking out of
dream into recognition of his role. Helen Vendler reminds us
that, 'Once again, in this play, the question of "Leda and the
Swan" is implicitly asked: what knowledge remains in the mind
as the residue of possession by the Daimon?'[19] In the play this
possession is suggested by the dance of the woman, and Cuchulain is lured and captured by it:

> The madness has laid hold upon him now,
> For he grows pale and staggers to his feet.

Yet Cuchulain's response is not submission, but conflict. He is
intent on mastery: 'Grey bird, you shall be perched upon my
wrist'. Although he has been lured from the well, his pursuit of
the dancer is a prelude to his pursuit of Aoife. His true role is
revealed. He can define himself, 'He comes! Cuchulain, son of
Sualtim, comes!' The Old Man is left in the waste land without
the compensating moment of revelation.

Harold Bloom remarks of this moment,

I am surprised always, in reading the play, at the extraordinary force of Cuchulain's call as he shoulders his spear. . . . The splendour of this would be lost if Cuchulain did not so sublimely put it in the third person. In context the effect is overpowering . . . .[20]

In my reading of the play, however, Cuchulain's words have a weak ring about them, a false, tinny bravado. I find little sense of tragic potential, little sense of the hero refusing to be overwhelmed. I feel that Cuchulain is dwarfed by the setting of the play as it is unfolded by the musicians. It is as if Cuchulain is lost in the immense power of the landscape in which he walks.

The musicians close the play with a reference to the hawk.

> I have found hateful eyes
> Among the desolate places. . . .

These desolate places leave us, as the play began, torn between two claims:

> I am content to perish;
> I am but a mouthful of sweet air

and 'Obscurity of strife'. These two elements are both part of the tragic encounter. Cuchulain, in choosing that brave folly ('Folly alone I cherish'), has also chosen a bitter wisdom:

> He has lost what may not be found
> Till men heap his burial mound
> And all the history ends.

What dominates this play is place. It is not, to my mind, the full abundance of the tragic moment that we feel, but its penury. We feel a sense of loss: 'Who but an idiot would praise / A withered tree?' In 'The Tragic Theatre' Yeats had written of the tragic hero that in his greatest moments 'all is lyricism, unmixed passion, "the integrity of fire"' (*E&I*, p. 240). Yeats, in his attempts to realise that integrity, comes up with something too thin in Cuchulain's expression in this play. What he does, however, is create a landscape for the tragic moment to which he will refer us constantly, both in his plays and in his poetry, from this point onwards.

The Only Jealousy of Emer (CPL, pp. 281–96) could well be
described as a baffling and obscure piece of work. Yeats's notes
on it show him to be working on the first draft of *A Vision,* here
referred to as the Robartes papers:

> In writing these little plays I knew that I was creating some-
> thing which could only fully succeed in a civilisation very
> unlike ours. I think they should be written for some country
> where all classes share in a half-mythological, half-philos-
> ophical folk-belief which the writer and his small audience lift
> into a new subtlety. . . . I have now found all the mythology
> and philosophy I need in the papers of my old friend and rival,
> Robartes.   (*VPl,* p. 566)

The play will require a look at *A Vision,* to explain its reference to
the fifteenth phase of ideal beauty and to the twelfth phase,
indicative of the hero. The problems, however, do not end here.
We shall have to look at Yeats's later prose version, *Fighting the
Waves* (1929), to see how it alters or clarifies certain of the play's
themes.

But the main problem posed by this play concerns a triangle of
emotional claims for sympathy from the audience. Cuchulain,
Emer and Fand all claim the central role. Helen Vendler dismisses the claims of Emer. The poet's intention was not, she argues,
to have us prefer Emer to Fand. The central conflict is between
Cuchulain and Fand. She warns us,

> So far as I can judge, the average reader sees *Emer* as a play
> about a selfless wife, a weak and straying husband, and a
> wicked temptress. Moral norms coerce this reader into ap-
> proval of Emer, condemnation of Cuchulain, and dislike of
> Fand, but it is important, I think, not to impose alien moral
> norms on these plays while interpreting them.[21]

Harold Bloom sees the problem in less black-and-white terms.
The play is not simply a battle between Cuchulain and Fand,
but a battle between the daimonic world and the human world,
with all the ambiguities we met in *At the Hawk's Well.* He also allies
the play with Yeats's marriage and possible regret for Maud
Gonne. The play is not coherent, he argues: 'we cannot know

whether to wish Cuchulain to end with Fand, or with his wife and mistress, whether he ought to belong to the condition of Fire or to the Terrestrial Condition'.[22] I feel that we have to recognise with Bloom that such a dilemma exists, that we are torn in different ways and therefore I cannot agree with Helen Vendler's thesis. It is not, however, that Fand is evil and Emer virtuous. We have to accommodate the claims of both.

For all these problems, I find this play richer and more satisfying than *At the Hawk's Well*. The twin images of the bereaved Emer and Fand haunt the play. It is in the twinning of these images that I find a partial answer to its problem. The play opens with a song in which Yeats evokes the fifteenth phase of the moon, in terms of beauty:

> A woman's beauty is like a white
> Frail bird, like a white sea-bird alone
> At daybreak after stormy night . . .
> A sudden storm, and it was thrown
> Between dark furrows upon the ploughed land.
> How many centuries spent
> The sedentary soul
> In toils of measurement
> Beyond eagle or mole,
> Beyond hearing or seeing,
> Or Archimedes' guess,
> To raise into being
> That loveliness?

In his notes on the play Yeats describes 'the invisible fifteenth incarnation [as] that of the greatest possible bodily beauty and those of the fourteenth and sixteenth incarnations, those of the greatest beauty visible to human eyes'. The fifteenth incarnation is described as the full moon, the complete triumph of the subjective nature. Physical beauty is described as 'the result of emotional toil in past lives' (*VPl*, p. 566). The opening song transforms the difficult and obscure nature of Yeats's symbolism. Beauty is envisaged as miraculous, a gift of storm. Yet the apparent accident of its existence is belied by centuries of labour. The second stanza of the song likens beauty to an opalescent shell – exquisite, delicate and fragile:

> A strange, unserviceable thing,
> A fragile, exquisite, pale shell,
> That the vast troubled waters bring
> To the loud sands before the day has broken.

In *A Vision* Yeats refers to the fifteenth incarnation as a time of war ('Aphrodite rises from a stormy sea', pp. 267–8), and in these opening lines there is a sense of battle:

> What death? what discipline?
> What bonds no man could unbind,
> Being imagined within
> The labyrinth of the mind,
> What pursuing or fleeing,
> What wounds, what bloody press,
> Dragged into being
> This loveliness?

The action of the play attempts an answer. Emer and Fand are the protagonists and this sense of ideal beauty is shared between them.

In this play Yeats uses the same device of a black cloth as in *At the Hawk's Well*. Again the chorus sets the scene, blocking at either end the action of the play, relating the twin images of Emer and Fand. The chorus, however, does not appear in the main action of the play. It sets the scene in the mind's eye: 'a poor fisher's house', a man lying as if dead. It reiterates the image of storm and sea, 'the vast troubled waters':

> Beyond the open door the bitter sea,
> The shining, bitter sea, is crying out,
> (*singing*) White shell, white wing!
> I will not choose for my friend
> A frail, unserviceable thing
> That drifts and dreams, and but knows
> That waters are without end
> And that wind blows.

The chorus reminds us of the tensions in *At the Hawk's Well*, with its rival claims. We might note as well the effect of seeing this play in terms of the Cuchulain cycle. We are on Baile's strand. Now,

however, Yeats can use his chorus to define place. The play is a
continuation of Cuchulain's fight with the waves and it could be
argued that the play takes place under water, in Cuchulain's
mind.

The later prose version makes this link explicit. *Fighting the
Waves (VPl,* pp. 529–64) begins with a dance. The stage directions tell us,

> *There is a curtain with a wave pattern. A man wearing the Cuchulain
> mask enters from one side with a sword and shield. He dances a dance
> which represents a man fighting the waves. The waves may be represented
> by other dancers: in his frenzy he supposes the waves to be his enemies:
> gradually he sinks down as if overcome, then fixes his eyes with a
> cataleptic stare upon some imaginary distant object. The stage becomes
> dark, and when the light returns it is empty.*

This dance is balanced with the dance of Fand at the end of the
play. The use of mask in both versions shows how Yeats's use of
the mask technique has developed. There now exists a recognisable Cuchulain mask. The audience is expected not only to
recognise this face, but also to be familiar with the story of *On
Baile's Strand.* Yeats is working within a mythology which should
be familiar to his audience already. The mask, however, is used
not merely to distance us from the everyday world, but also for
disguise. And Fand's mask, as we shall see, is a mask in the sense
I discussed with reference to 'Anima Hominis' – a quasi-
religious emblem.

As *The Only Jealousy of Emer* unfolds, Yeats uses Emer and
Eithne Inguba to explain the plot. This is a stilted device and
could have been better handled by the chorus. Eithne is Emer's
only earthly rival, whom she is prepared to accept because of the
hope that Cuchulain will one day return to her. She and Eithne
are to share in winning Cuchulain back from the sea. While
Eithne speaks to him, Emer builds up the fire to ward off the
power of the sea, recalling the song in *On Baile's Strand*:

> Old Manannan's unbridled horses come
> Out of the sea, and on their backs his horsemen;
> But all the enchantments of the dreaming foam
> Dread the hearth-fire.

As in the earlier play, the song seems to evoke the power of the sea rather than to banish it. Bricriu, who has possessed himself of Cuchulain's body, using the Cuchulain mask for disguise, frightens Eithne away[23] Bricriu demands of Emer her one hope, that Cuchulain will one day return to her. This is her 'only jealousy'. Bricriu reveals the true figure of Cuchulain and invites Emer to become the audience of Cuchulain's encounter with Fand. In this way, we pass through two layers of perception to view the central conflict.

In the later prose version this battle is simply a dance. (*VPl*, p. 554). There is no debate:

> *The Woman of the Sidhe, Fand, moves around the crouching Ghost of Cuchulain . . . in a dance that grows gradually quicker as he awakes . . . . She is accompanied by string and flute and drum. Her mask and her clothes must suggest gold or bronze or brass and silver, so that she seems more an idol than a human being. This suggestion may be repeated in her movements. (CPl,* 291)[24]

These directions apply to both versions, but in the prose version the mask and dance movements are enough to suggest the conflict between man and anti-self. In the earlier version a highly complicated verbal battle takes place. This expresses ideas that receive fuller treatment in *A Vision*. Fand is seen in terms of the fifteenth incarnation, the full moon. Cuchulain recognises her in these terms:

> Who is it stands before me there
> Shedding such light from limb and hair
> As when the moon, complete at last
> With every labouring crescent past,
> And lonely with extreme delight
> Flings out upon the fifteenth night?

But Fand denies this: 'Because I long, I am not complete.' What Yeats suggests here, I think, is that the moment of tragedy must be a meeting between opposites. The supernatural is not sufficient of itself; it is the meeting between the two worlds which creates the moment of vision. Then, we need to see what Fand has to offer the hero. She offers him peace, but it is also oblivion:

When your mouth and my mouth meet
All my round shall be complete
Imagining all its circles run;
And there shall be oblivion
Even to quench Cuchulain's drouth . . . .

This is a retreat from conflict:

And shall I never know again
Intricacies of blind remorse?

Oblivion would be the end of the heroic role as announced and recognised by Cuchulain at the end of *At the Hawk's Well*. It would be the overwhelming of the hero by the waves he is fighting against. Cuchulain as a hero belongs to the twelfth incarnation or phase of the moon. In *A Vision* Yeats describes the hero as 'the man who overcomes himself, and so no longer needs others . . . . Solitude has been born at last, though solitude invaded and hard to defend' (pp. 127–8). The hero is pursued by accidents. If he meets these in the correct antithetical manner 'there is a noble extravagance, an overflowing fountain of personal life' (ibid.). His mask should be 'lonely', imperturbable, proud' (ibid.). His nature, on the other hand, is conscious of weakness, and his mask, solitude and pride are the only means of achieving his heroic stance. Fand is, in this sense, a temptress, since she offers release from conflict and solitude.

It is Emer's decision which returns Cuchulain to his heroic nature. Her action in renouncing his love places Emer curiously close to Fand, who has lost it. Emer too turns herself to stone. The concluding lines of the play, in which the musicians once more control and distance our reactions, are again complex. Do they refer to Emer? Do they refer to Fand? The dance which ends the later prose version clearly points to Fand. She dances

a dance which expresses her despair for the loss of Cuchulain. As before there may be other dancers who represent the waves. It is called, in order to balance the first dance, 'Fand mourns among the waves'. It is essentially a dance which symbolises, like water in the fortune-telling books, bitterness. As she takes her final pose of despair the Curtain falls.

(*VPl*, p. 564)

I think, however, that the bitterness with which the play ends also refers to Emer. Fand is Emer's anti-self, her opposite, perhaps her mask. Yeats suggests this reading in an introductory note to *Fighting the Waves*:

> 'Everything he loves must fly', everything he desires; Emer too must renounce desire, but there is another love, that which is like the man-at-arms in the Anglo-Saxon poem, 'doom-eager'. Young, we discover an opposite through our love; old, we discover our love through some opposite neither hate nor despair can destroy, because it is another self, a self that we have fled in vain.   (p. 571)

Emer finds her opposite in Fand. Fand's mask is doubly important. It is not only a theatrical technique, but the mask of tragedy. The only jealousy of Emer has been her discovery of this other self. In recognising herself in the waves of the sea, she is able to overcome the waves of the sea. In this way the closing lines of the play complement the opening. Where the first celebrate ideal beauty, its fragility and the cost at which it is born, the closing lines call us to view the tragedy which has made it possible.

Into the landscape of *At the Hawk's Well* with its sense of desolation, bitterness and defeat, Yeats introduces a corresponding drama. In addition, *The Only Jealousy of Emer* makes clear that the supernatural has no value on its own. It is when it is knit to the human and natural that we reach the moment of tragic recognition. At the end Fand is both inhuman and human. Seen in relation to Emer, she shows us the moment described in 'Anima Hominis' when we know 'another's breath' breathing within our own. The closing lines of the play refer us to the opposition between Emer and Fand, who become one another. Their battle may be seen to take place, as does the entire action of the play, within Cuchulain's trance, under water:

> Why does your heart beat thus?
> Plain to be understood,
> I have met in a man's house
> A statue of solitude,
> Moving there and walking;
> Its strange heart beating fast

For all our talking.
O still that heart at last.

With *The Dreaming of the Bones* we return to a close following of the Noh theatre. The model is one of the most accessible of the plays translated by Fenellosa, *Nishikigi*. David Clark, in his study of the play, refers us to source material in another Noh play where a girl is trapped in a hell of her own making, unable to forgive herself.[25] Clark argues that Diarmuid and Dervogilla's guilt – and the Young Man's response to it – exhibits the same dilemma, that of a country unable to forgive itself. I should like to draw attention briefly to *Nishikigi*[26] because of its structure, which Yeats follows very closely but turns on its heels. The Japanese play shares characteristics common to all Noh plays. A place is imbued with a sense of awe. A wandering figure, here a priest, describes the scene to us. He is known as the *waki*. He is making a journey and, by asking directions, is able to evoke a picture of the landscape. The main story is acted out before the *waki* as an interior play. As common in the Noh, the protagonists are ghosts. We are distanced from them. These ghosts, the *tshite* or male hero and the *tsure* or heroine, underline at once the major image of the play, that of the unwoven cloth that is the cause of their separation. Their grief is like the tangled thread of the cloth *hosonumo*, 'Tangled we are entangled. Whose fault was it, dear? Tangled up as the grass patterns are tangled up in this coarse cloth.' The chorus intercedes, stating and restating these images of separation. Voices question, echo and interpret each other. The *waki* does not at once recognise that the two protagonists are ghosts. They tell their story to him as of strangers and they lead him to the place where the story was enacted:

We have spent the whole day until dusk
Pushing aside the grass
From the overgrown way at Kefu,
And we are not yet come to the cave.

The chorus describes the fall of night, the tangled flowers and undergrowth that surround the cave. In this place the two lovers reveal their true identity and re-enact their tale before the *waki*. But now, through his intervention, they can meet and the play closes with a dance of betrothal, a celebration: 'Tread out the

dance / Tread out the dance and bring music.' As the play ends
the lovers disappear, leaving the stage empty but for the *waki*, as
if it had all been illusion:

> There is nothing here but this cave in the field's midst.
> Today's wind moves in the pines;
> A wild place, unlit, and unfilled.

Yet in this play wrongs have been righted. There is a joyful
resolution. A reading of *Nishikigi* makes *The Dreaming of the Bones*
more poignant:

> Now is there meeting between us,
> Between us who were until now
> In life and in after-life, kept apart.
> A dream bridge over wild grass . . . .
>
> It is a good service you have done, sir,
> A service that spreads in two worlds,
> And binds up an ancient love
> That was stretched out between them.

In Yeats's play it is guilt and the refusal of mercy which spread
into two worlds.

Yeats's notes on his play show his indebtedness to the Noh,
but also to ideas which he is exploring in the early days of *A
Vision*:

> The conception of the play is derived from the world-wide
> belief that the dead dream back, for a certain time, through
> the more personal thoughts and deeds of life . . . and there is
> precisely the same thought in a Japanese 'Noh' play.
>
> (*VPl*, p. 777)

The lovers in Yeats's play 'have lost themselves in a different but
still self-created winding of the labyrinth of conscience' (ibid.).
Yeats gives his version of the *waki* greater involvement in the
action and, since the *waki* stands in some measure for the
audience, we must share that greater involvement. This means
that we too are asked to respond to the guilt and suffering of the
lovers. In the Irish context of the play, the dreaming back of the

ghosts becomes not only their personal tragedy, but the history of Ireland. The treatment of Ireland is far more complex than, for example, that we meet in *Cathleen ni Houlihan*. In some respects the situation is reversed. In that play Ireland in the guise of the Young/Old Woman comes from the other or ghostly world, destroying security and normality. Now Ireland as a political force is represented by the Young Man's normality and his suspicion of this other world. Ireland is presented to us in this play in several different perspectives or guises. The landscape with its barren and desolate imagery recalls a remark which Yeats notes in the essay 'First Principles' of 1904: 'A nation is the heroic theme we follow, a mourning wasted land its moving spirit; the impersonal assumes personality for us' (*E*, p. 142). Men and women play a subordinate role. This vision of Ireland reflects the ambiguities of Yeats's response to the Easter Rising – its fanaticism transforming the heart to stone, to something grotesque and less than human.

The Dreaming of the Bones (*CPl*, pp. 433–45) is entirely different from the light, inconsequentially joyous *Nishikigi*. But Yeats follows its form almost exactly. The techniques of the Noh are brought into full and effective play. For the first time the chorus is used throughout the play. The ghosts too distance themselves, by telling their own story as of strangers and by presenting a dance. Whereas in *At the Hawk's Well* and *The Only Jealousy of Emer* there was a tendency for the central characters to contradict the tone of the chorus, operating as if they belonged in the more naturalistic structure of the earlier plays, there is, here, a complete unity of tone.

The play begins with the unfolding and folding of a cloth, but, when the chorus begins to create the landscape, more emphasis is placed on the response of the spectators. We are made to feel the eerie sensations of the mountain, to respond to the desolation of the place as if we were there:

> Why does my heart beat so?
> Did not a shadow pass?
> It passed but a moment ago.

The countless dead already seem to inhabit the scene as the chorus describes its loneliness:

> Birds cry, they cry their loneliness.
> Even the sunlight can be lonely here,
> Even hot noon is lonely.

The Young Man explains himself to the two strangers and then listens as they take over the action of the play, describing the terrors to which he will be prey. The youth is presented as a man of action, but also one opposed to the antithetical or subjective vision. For all that he is on the run, he belongs to the normal or surface world. He has no fear, for 'They cannot put me into gaol or shoot me'. His perception is naïve.

Yeats has now mastered the conventions of the Noh. Here, in making the Young Man climb under the guidance of the two strangers, he uses the chorus to describe the journey and the place. Each circuit of the stage, signifying part of the journey, interrupts the action and builds up tension and excitement. The chorus sets up a cry of terror:

> Why should the heart take fright?
> What sets it beating so?
> The bitter sweetness of the night
> Has made it but a lonely thing.

The themes of the play are again and again reiterated: the sense of the eerie, the wildness of the place with its ragged thorn trees, the cry of the 'cat-headed' bird and the sense of the past reliving itself:

> My head is in a cloud;
> I'd let the whole world go;
> My rascal heart is proud
> Remembering and remembering.

The song comes to a climax like a scream. It takes us both to the hill-top and right out of the everyday world:

> The dreaming bones cry out
> Because the night winds blow
> And heaven's a cloudy blot.
> Calamity can have its fling.

Calamity hangs over the play. Each burst of song ends with a hysterical cry for daylight and release:

> Red bird of March, begin to crow!
> Up with the neck and clap the wing,
> Red cock, and crow!

Looking down from the summit of the hill, and having passed through a period of initiation to this eerie, supernatural world, the Young Man sees Ireland spread out before him, all in devastation:

> Is there no house
> Famous for sanctity or architectural beauty
> In Clare or Kerry, or in all wide Connacht,
> The enemy has not unroofed?

His range of vision is limited. He is slow to respond to the description given by the strangers of the sufferings of the dead. There are three levels of vision before us, or three overlapping landscapes: first the landscape created by the staging of the play; next the political landscape of Ireland as seen by the Young Man; and finally the spiritual or daimonic landscape of the dead. Last to be revealed is the identity of the strangers. They first tell him of themselves, teaching him to see beyond his limited and lurid vision of an after-life:

> I have heard that there are souls
> Who, having sinned after a monstrous fashion,
> Take on them, being dead, a monstrous image
> To drive the living should they meet its face,
> Crazy . . . .

Dervogilla explains another kind of penance:

> These have no thought but love; nor any joy
> But that upon the instant when their penance
> Draws to its height, and when two hearts are wrung
> Nearest to breaking, if hearts of shadows break,
> His eyes can mix with hers; nor any pang
> That is so bitter as that double glance,
> Being accursed. . . .

> The memory of their crime flows up between
> And drives them apart.

Their landscape is revealed: 'they are but shadows, / Hovering between a thorn-tree and a stone'.

But the Young Man denies their plea for mercy. His vision is still limited to the political landscape: 'That town had lain / But for the pair that you would have me pardon'. David Clark puts the discrepancy of vision differently. He tells us,

> The speeches of the ghosts continually dim the immediacy of the landscape, even while describing it. They put a veil before its objective reality. The Young Man's speeches are true to the clear outlines of the landscape, but not always to its tide of passionate associations.[27]

My argument is that these passionate associations reveal another landscape beyond the limits of his. His landscape is not the one of objective reality, but the landscape of a political vision. These visions finally coincide when the Young Man at last recognises the true identity of the strangers and describes their dance. It is on his report that we are able to see it. It is a complete reversal of the joyous dance which ends *Nishikigi*:

> Why do you dance?
> Why do you gaze, and with so passionate eyes,
> One on the other; and then turn away,
> Covering your eyes, and weave it in a dance?

We feel the presence of history here, but it is the history of suffering and remorse that holds us closer than the Young Man's account of seven hundred years. We listen to the lovers: 'Seven hundred years our lips have never met.' But the Young Man cannot forgive them. He opens up the prospect of another seven hundred years of suffering. He returns to the limits of his own political vision:

> I had almost yielded and forgiven it all –
> Terrible the temptation and the place!

The Dreaming of the Bones is, I should argue, the most theatrically effective of Yeats's dance plays. The use of the Young Man as guide, the circuits of the stage which depict the journey to the mountain peak, the climax of the play as we are confronted with the alien world of the dead – these allow Yeats to focus on the moment of vision. In *The Words upon the Window-Pane* (1934) Yeats will return to this juxtaposition between two worlds, but there we are allowed only a glimpse, as into a private world. Here we are forced to participate in the Young Man's rejection of mercy, forced to participate in the remorse which accompanies Diarmuid and Dervogilla in the recognition of their guilt. The play depicts a purgatorial landscape[28] in terms of barren rock and ruined architecture. This is, as I have suggested, the archetypal landscape or setting for Yeatsian tragedy. It is 'the place of stone', the wilderness where we confront darkness and are thus given the light of vision, however painful. The dance which closes the play is arguably the most evocative of Yeats's images of tragedy, depicting as it does the eternal separation of lover and beloved. Their very closeness one to the other intensifies their distance from each other. They are trapped within sight and arm's length of their desire, yet eternally thwarted of its attainment.

The differences between Yeats's play and his model are here particularly apparent. Having looked at Yeats's use of Noh theatre techniques, we should look at where he digresses from the Noh model. Richard Taylor summarises Yeats's affinities with the Noh:

> sensuous rhythms and patterns of natural images are so arranged and ordered as to charge objective images with pure and intense emotion and to disclose by direct correspondence the pattern of ideal order which existed beyond time. Fenellosa understood Nō as ritual rather than drama; not an imitation of life, but rather a transfiguration of its forms through human imagination in which universal antitheses are synthesized and reconciled.[29]

Taylor goes on to describe how, in the Noh, the human world with all its pain and confusion is bounded by a higher order and how the Noh cycle depicts 'universal order, a golden chain by which the human condition is reconciled with spiritual values. . . . [The] spiritual unity of beauty and moral action are revealed.'[30] Though we find the transfiguration of life in Yeats's plays, we do not find universal order. The general tone is of loss rather than joy. Taylor sees ritual drama, such as that of the Noh, as militating against tragic statement:

> Although tragic implications may figure in ritual drama as in the case of *The Bacchae* or *Samson Agonistes*, the importance of the form is in the revelation of 'what is' or 'what should be' in terms of the public good, a demonstration of the touchstone and ordering principle on which the stability of the community rests.[31]

Yeats does not in fact believe in the ultimate stability of the community. He rejects solutions and this is clear throughout his work. Indeed the East, in which we may include these Noh plays, is frequently rejected by Yeats precisely because of this sense of resolved conflict.[32] Yeats's definition of tragedy and tragic joy rejects any idea of the reconciliation of opposites. As with Blake, the existence of any quality presupposes its opposite. There is always conflict, and the moment of tragic joy, though it may contain a glimpse of reconciliation, is really a poised tension, a bracing, a refusal to be overwhelmed. When Yeats brings in the supernatural it is never to resolve his plot, to end the agony, but rather to increase it. The Sidhe stand for the unseen, the anti-self, the world of the dead, the world of fears that must be encountered by the hero. For the Yeatsian hero there is no way out.

Yeats's plays give us an introduction to three major aspects of his expression of tragedy. First is his concentration on the heightened tragic moment, which is seen as a conflict between two worlds. The hero is always seen in conflict with another self, as Cuchulain with hawk-woman or Emer with Fand. Writing of Swedenborg, Yeats tells us of his discovery: 'we are each in the midst of a group of associated spirits who sleep when we sleep and become the *dramatis personae* of our dreams, and are always the other will that wrestles with our thought shaping it to our despite' (*E*, p. 37). In the essay 'Anima Hominis' that conflict is sharpened and related to the poet's battle with his muse:

> I sometimes fence for half an hour at the day's end and when I close my eyes upon the pillow I see a foil playing before me, the button to my face. We meet always in the deep of the

mind, whatever our work, wherever our reverie carries us, that other Will.   (*M*, p. 337)

The second aspect we meet in these plays is a doctrine of ideal beauty and the joy and threat it harbours. In poems such as 'A Prayer for my Daughter' and 'Among School Children', Yeats will explore the murderous and merciful nature of beauty. It is both the goal and curse of the poet and is related to the other-world figures of the Sidhe.

Thirdly, and, I should argue, most significantly, we enter a landscape which evokes an atmosphere of despair, terror, futility and loss. Like the dance of Diarmuid and Dervogilla, it speaks of thwarted desire and frustration. Like the closing song in *The Only Jealousy of Emer*, it captures the moment when two worlds meet. These plays outline the dark side of that encounter. They show little of the joy and fullness which we meet in many of Yeats's poems. But, like the phases of the moon in *A Vision*, this tragic landscape provides a touchstone to which Yeats will both explicitly and implicitly refer us.

3 A Tragic Universe: The Framework of *A Vision*

In the last chapter we saw how Yeats's dance plays concentrate attention on a visionary encounter between two worlds, the natural and supernatural. The supernatural, appearing as the Sidhe, reveals the beautiful and terrible figure of the Muse, the anti-self, the Daimon, a force hostile or indifferent to man, yet essential to his moment of truth and tragic recognition. In these plays we saw how Yeats creates a landscape which echoes and embodies emotional states of terror, futility and loss and which captures the paradoxical moment of agony and ecstasy where tragic vision is attained. The plays concentrate on the dark side of tragedy. Their landscape mirrors the transformation of abundance to penury which is for Yeats characteristic of the tragic moment. We are led, as Yeats remarks of Synge (*E&I*, p. 339), to the light of a judgement day, to an apocalyptic moment. In this chapter I draw attention to *A Vision*, in which the idea of apocalypse dominates. I argue that this vision, revelation or apocalypse is a tragic one, and my aim in this chapter is to show how Yeats's system provides a framework or world-picture in which tragedy is inevitable, is an expression of reality itself.

A Vision is undoubtedly dangerous ground to travel over and it is easy to get lost in a maze of bizarre jargon. Helen Vendler writes of Yeats's customary 'solemn gravity' in this work, a gravity which 'most of his commentators have imitated'. She comments,

> Parts of *A Vision* deserve gravity, but others must be taken with a grain of salt, and not even the most admiring critic can swallow *A Vision* whole. But the choice is not between accepting the 'mystic geometry' wholesale and shrugging it off as one of Yeats's dotages. There is a middle course, and that is to see *A Vision* as a symbolic statement, somewhat cluttered up with

psychic paraphernalia, which yields itself quite well to reasonable interpretation.[1]

Though my reading of *A Vision* differs from Helen Vendler's, as I shall show, her remarks seem to me helpful. My reading of *A Vision* in terms of a tragic understanding of reality seems to me a 'reasonable interpretation' of its 'symbolic statement'. Many studies of *A Vision* provide commentary on and exploration of the mechanics of Yeats's system. The most useful and enlightening of these include Helen Vendler's study and Thomas Whitaker's *Swan and Shadow*,[2] and I discuss their response to Yeats's system later in this chapter. At the risk of oversimplifying a complex and also frustrating work, I am assuming some acquaintance with *A Vision* and will concentrate on those aspects of it which are pertinent to tragic vision.

A Vision expresses four related ideas which are central to the tragic vision in Yeats. The first concerns its title. Yeats's system is vision, apocalypse, revelation, judgement day. We need to explore how apocalypse and tragedy relate to each other. The first section of this chapter explores critical reaction to Yeats's system, reaction which highlights this problem. I also explore the influence of two of *A Vision's* precursors, Nietzsche and Castiglione. These help define the nature of Yeats's tragic vision. I begin the section with two poems, 'The Cold Heaven' and 'The Magi', which introduce us to the idea of tragic apocalypse.

The second area of *A Vision* central to tragic vision is its delineation of two diametrically opposed states of being, the Vision of Evil and Unity of Being, or phase one and phase fifteen of Yeats's system. For Yeats, tragic vision is a fusion of these two extremes. The second section of this chapter explores these two states which recur throughout Yeats's work. I look at the poem 'The Double Vision of Michael Robartes' to show how these two states confine man within a tragic process.

A third area of *A Vision* defines and explores the nature of the tragic encounter between man and his opposite. This encounter, one of tortuous conflict, leads toward a tragic vision which is also truth, reality itself. Although the paraphernalia of *A Vision* – 'Faculties', 'Principles', 'Mask' and 'Daimon' – can be off-putting, we find at the core of Yeats's system the idea of life as a necessary confrontation between opposites. Life is experienced as extreme tension between object of desire and frustration of desire, between terror and delight, between form and chaos, between art and experience.

Finally, and running through all these areas, we have the cyclical nature of Yeats's system, which ensures a pessimistic vision of life. Neither for the individual nor for the civilisation to which he belongs can there be any perfection now or in the future. Moments of felicity and even ecstasy there are, but they are spasmodic and rare. We shall explore these moments, which are the primary expression of tragic joy, and their relationship to the cyclical movement which is man's experience of life. The third section of this chapter explores Yeats's system as it relates to historical cycle and the moment of apocalyptic transformation when a new cycle dawns. I examine two poems, 'The Second Coming' and 'Leda and the Swan', to show how Yeats envisages the historical cycle as part of the human and tragic situation. In conclusion, I examine the poem 'I see Phantoms of Hatred and of the Heart's Fullness and of the Coming Emptiness'.

I

'The Cold Heaven' introduces us to vision as tragic apocalypse. This is a poem of revelation. If we compare it with the earlier treatment of vision in, for example, 'The Secret Rose', we see that Yeats is now redefining vision, and making it closer to 'a representation of what actually exists really and unchangeably' (*E&I*, p. 116). In 'The Secret Rose' (*CP*, pp. 77–8) the central vision is of beauty:

> A woman of so shining loveliness
> That men threshed corn at midnight by a tress . . . .

But this illumination evokes two contradictory responses. The poem begins with an identification of the quest for beauty with sleep. Those who have attained vision are seen as 'beyond the stir / And tumult of defeated dreams' and 'heavy with the sleep / Men have named beauty'. The poem, however, concludes with a plea for turbulence and apocalyptic destruction:

> When shall the stars be blown about the sky
> Like the sparks blown out of a smithy, and die?

In 'The Cold Heaven' (*CP*, p. 140) that contradiction has vanished. Vision has nothing now to do with dreamy sleep, everything to do with turbulence. Vision is now terrible, clear-eyed and final as a last judgement. It is the vision of loss. The woman, whether Rose, Muse or beloved, is now seen as unattainable. The landscape is that of the dance plays, the landscape of deprivation. The poem strikes us as a blast of cold air. The whole universe – of the cold heaven – is the setting. But what distinguishes the poem from the dance plays is its tone of ecstatic revelation,

> Suddenly I saw the cold and rook-delighting heaven
> That seemed as though ice burned and was but the more
>   ice. . . .

We are carried beyond 'every casual thought of that and this' until, with the poet, nothing is left us but memories 'of love crossed long ago'. Imagination, heart, sense and reason are all compelled to confront this one certainty, purged into vision, 'Until I cried and trembled and rocked to and fro / Riddled with light'. Harold Bloom, in his study *Yeats*, comments on the suggestive use of the last phrase 'with its play on "riddled", as though the light of the cold heaven were the light of Maud Gonne's beautiful presence and spirit, at once an arrow . . . and a Sphinx'.[3] Maud Gonne here takes on the role of Muse, and the poem suggests the relationship between man and Daimon which Yeats will develop in *A Vision*. In 'The Cold Heaven' Yeats is brought face to face with his Daimon, Muse or anti-self. The meeting is both ecstatic and terrifying. The dominant image is one of violent transfiguration:

> Ah! when the ghost begins to quicken,
> Confusion of the death-bed over, is it sent
> Out naked on the roads, as the books say, and stricken
> By the injustice of the skies for punishment?

The poem gives us a universe where there is no ultimate peace, no dreamy sleep, only a continuation of conflict, loss and remorse. What the poem achieves, confronted by this hideous and unrelenting universe, is an energetic enactment of conflict. As in the dance plays this exuberant energy is transformed into its

opposite, into nakedness. Yeats here universalises the experience
of the individual man and his Daimon. The pain of the unre-
quited lover is deepened into the nakedness of absolute loss. At
the same time the abstract of the universe, which will later be
symbolised in the mathematical figures of *A Vision*, is directly
experienced as human and individual fate. The universe presented 'as the books say' is proved and lived in the individual
life. 'The Cold Heaven' illustrates the moment when we see life as
tragedy and hence, according to Yeats, begin to live (*A*, p. 189).

'The Magi' (*CP*, p. 141) explores the tragic universe which
makes the tragic vision of life inescapable. It is concerned with
'the injustice of the skies' we met in 'The Cold Heaven'. In the
world dominated by the Magi, man is utterly helpless. Yeats's
notes link 'The Magi' with 'The Dolls'. In 'The Dolls' (*CP*, pp.
141–2) abstraction and purity dominate, disdaining the 'fury
and mire' of human blood:

> The man and the woman bring
> Hither, to our disgrace,
> A noisy and filthy thing.

Yeats notes of this poem how our thought is 'frozen into "something other than human life"'. The vision which inspires 'The
Magi' is a reaction to 'those enraged dolls': 'I looked up one day
into the blue of the sky, and suddenly imagined, as if lost in the
blue of the sky, stiff figures in procession. I remembered that
they were the habitual image suggested by blue sky . . . (*CP*,
p. 531). The blue sky, personified in the figures of the Magi,
becomes a lid on the world, the prison in which man is trapped.
The Magi speak with a calm, cold certainty:

> Now as at all times I can see in the mind's eye,
> In their stiff, painted clothes, the pale unsatisfied
>   ones . . . .

The conflict hinted at in 'The Dolls' is now centred on power.
The Magi of the poem dominate. They are also immutable.
They

> Appear and disappear in the blue depths of the sky
> With all their ancient faces like rain-beaten stones,

And all their helms of silver hovering side by side,
And all their eyes still fixed . . . .

They blend indifference and curiosity, as if conducting an experiment. These figures represent the cyclical pattern within which man is bound. They turn the wheels of history from era to era:

> hoping to find once more,
> Being by Calvary's turbulence unsatisfied,
> The uncontrollable mystery on the bestial floor.

The two poems 'The Cold Heaven' and 'The Magi', relating the startling moment of tragic vision and the cyclical universe in which man is trapped, reflect Yeats's characteristic use of two modes of vision: the experienced or personal, and the panoramic or general. They are a useful introduction to the system of *A Vision* and its double vision of terror and delight.

In reading Yeats's system as a tragic vision, I have taken into account two major critical responses. The first response, most clearly articulated in Helen Vendler's *Yeats's 'Vision' and the Later Plays*,[4] sees *A Vision* as a poetics. At its broadest her argument allows that 'there are many other things in these books of *A Vision*, but the central spindle of each book seems to be a poetic one, around which Yeats winds endless relevant and irrelevant threads'.[5] She corrects one critical oversight. When Yeats tells us that the Instructors came to give him 'metaphors for poetry', she argues that 'their statement is generally interpreted to mean that *A Vision* contained metaphors (such as gyres) that could be used in a poetic way. A truer interpretation might be to say that all of *A Vision* is a series of metaphorical statements about poetry'.[6] Melchiori, in his study of Yeats, takes a similar line of approach. He argues that the poet will be searching all the time, if unconsciously, 'for the nature of poetry and the mode of its creation'.[7] Any systems of philosophy or cosmology or politics, though in themselves they may be wild or even criminal, will, when considered 'as statements about the nature of the poetic process', be 'substantially true'.[8] This approach I accept as broadly true, and in this context Helen Vendler's examination of *A Vision* is particularly enlightening, but still begs a question. If the elaborate system Yeats presents is a metaphor for poetic composition, what does it tell us about poetry? Harold Bloom, whose response to *A Vision* I shall examine shortly, asks this question: 'What precisely is Yeats trying to say about human life, and has he found an adequate image for his insight, if it is one?'[9] To the argument is now introduced the question of value and morality. The major omission we meet in Helen Vendler's study of Yeats's system concerns this area. She has difficulties in accommodating Yeats's definition and use of the word 'evil', for example, and rapidly dismisses it as of little relevance.[10]

The second major critical response concentrates to a much greater extent on questions of value. This response defines *A Vision* as apocalyptic and as 'serious and brilliant philosophy of history'.[11] But, though there is some agreement on definitions, reaction is sharply divided. Whitaker in his study *Swan and Shadow* is a staunch defender of Yeats's system and its implications, while Harold Bloom, for example, vehemently disapproves of it. Central in these reactions is the question of evil and the implications of a cyclical system for an ethical stance.

Whitaker sees *A Vision* as part of Yeats's long debate with an anti-self, which includes the non-created world of history – that is, a world not created by the poet. History is seen as an *alter ego*, 'a mysterious interlocutor',[12] who may sometimes reflect the poet and sometimes oppose him: 'He could endow it with his own imaginative life . . . he could also expect it to disclose all that he sought, all that seemed contrary to his own conscious state, all that lurked in his own depths, unmeasured and un-declared.'[13] For Whitaker this is predominantly a voyage of discov-ery which leads the poet 'toward an awareness of his own more comprehensive nature and toward a passionate self-judgement that was also a judgement of the dominant qualities of his time'.[14] This debate with history reflects, for Whitaker, gnostic or theosophical vision. According to such vision the world 'at the beginning of time (which is to say, at every moment)',[15] is created by the reflection of God. Thus creation is also a fall, a shadow, even 'the dark yet glittering inversion of God – the Dragon, the Serpent himself'.[16] Man is a microcosm of this world. The paradox of such a vision is that, in this fallen world, shadow or serpent can be a means of redemption:

> Man darkly discerns in all that is 'evil', all that is 'other', his antithetical *daimon*, a hidden manifestation of God or of his deeper self. If he makes the heroic effort to open himself to the

fullness of experience, he may be led by that anti-self toward an understanding of both microcosm and macrocosm.[17]

The climax of such an effort is 'a tragic joy born not of escape from the human condition but of a fullness of self-knowledge and self-judgement'.[18] The emphasis is on fullness, totality and completion. Whitaker is intent on attempting to justify Yeats's moral position. He is aware of the dangers of Yeats's position, which seeks 'to reconcile Christ and Lucifer, the self-giving and the self-asserting'.[19] In such a position how can one distinguish between good and evil? Whitaker argues that Yeats, by discovering 'the Dionysian abyss'[20] within himself, can therefore 'render and judge an evil that can be fully known only by one who has conversed with an interior Lucifer'.[21] For Whitaker, Yeats's apocalypse, 'an image of wholeness transcending the fragmented temporal world and self',[22] 'could be nothing other than a full rendering of the opposites within that world and self'.[23] Such an exploration, he argues, leads not to the elimination of the concepts 'right' and 'wrong', 'but to the agony and exhilaration of self-knowledge'.[24] Whitaker allows that this is an 'ambiguous way of ethical action',[25] but, significantly, he sees it as a means for the poet 'to transform himself into his own tragic character': 'Like his own image of Parnell, "Through Jonathan Swift's dark groove he passed, and there / Plucked bitter wisdom that enriched his blood." '[29] He sees Yeats as 'translating into individual reality the ruinous forces of our time'.[27]

Harold Bloom, in his study *Yeats*, takes a very different line on the question of Yeats's treatment of ethics. For him, Yeats comes close not to translating, but to provoking and perpetrating, 'the ruinous forces of our time'. The introductory paragraphs to his discussion of *A Vision* are almost entirely concerned with a moral condemnation of Yeats's system. In response to those critics who see *A Vision* as a culminating work, he assents grimly, 'I am afraid that it is.'[28] He turns aside from Helen Vendler's thesis with a reluctant 'I wish that this were true.'[29] He argues that Yeats's system must be judged in terms of his poetic tradition, 'his masters in vision'.[30] He concludes his preamble to *A Vision* with a magnificent display of moral disapproval:

Yeats's mythology has affinities, a few deliberate, many accidental, with dark crankeries too readily available elsewhere, most massively in the arcane speculations of Jung and his cohorts. Jung is a bad Romantic poet, Yeats a great one who suffered, in *A Vision*, a failure of vision. Failures in vision can be judged, and measured, only against vision . . . .[31]

For Harold Bloom the failure of Yeats's vision lies first in a misreading of Blake. He shows how in the commentary on Blake by Yeats and Ellis we can find the seeds of Yeats's primary and antithetical man. Yeats takes two poles, 'the personal and the impersonal or, as Blake preferred to call them, the limit of contraction and the unlimited expansion'[32]:

> When we act from the personal we tend to bind our conscious-
> ness down as to a fiery centre. When, on the other hand, we
> allow our imagination to expand away from this egoistic
> mood, we become vehicles for the universal thought and
> merge in the universal mood.[33]

From this point onwards, however, Blake and Yeats are seen to diverge. Yeats sees in the fallen world a shadow or anti-self which may lead to a moment of unity. He does not 'exorcise' this shadow. Bloom argues that Yeats refuses to see that Blake has made a very different choice:

> To Blake the shadow or serpent was a self-hood, but not the
> 'other' or creative self; it was the stifler or Covering Cherub,
> the separating or inhibiting force of nature and history, sanc-
> tified by an inadequate version of reason, and by an unjust
> organization of society.[34]

Yeats felt that this shadow could have two purposes or mean-ings, that it could be both 'a satanic hindrance' from freedom and a means by which freedom could be made 'visible in symbol and representative form'.[35] Bloom points out that Yeats inter-prets a dialectical figure as a cyclical one and consequently finds 'the *daimonic* where Blake saw the demonic, the genuine death of the imagination'.[36]

Investigating Yeats's cyclical figure further, Bloom finds that underlying the system is 'a hidden divinity' neither Christian nor Romantic, 'a composite God', the 'god of process', 'a dehumanising divinity'.[37] There is no sign of Blake's Human Form Divine, no sign of Shelley's Restored man. Instead Bloom argues that Yeats attempts to set up 'a new naturalist religion' and seeks 'to save man by teaching him . . . the supposedly curative powers of phantasmagoria'.[38] I am not myself sure that Yeats sets out to save anyone in *A Vision*. Bloom argues that.

> The starting-point of *A Vision* is Yeats's consciousness of man's fall into division, and his determination to restore man to unity, but even in that starting-point the vision of man has diminished, and we need to ask at what price the restoration to unity is to be bought.[39]

Certainly the starting-point is a sense of division, and the fifteenth phase is held against this as an ideal of unity. Certainly the price is high. It is the cost of the tragic gesture. But Yeats attempts no final solution or ultimate redemption. The only solution possible is a momentary glimpse of unity. Bloom accurately notes the tendency of Yeats's system to become entirely deterministic: 'Yeats's gyres rise . . . out of an entirely cyclic movement that he held to be present in every human consciousness, a movement of pure process . . . .'[40] But he goes on further and appears to recognise the implications behind such a system. Yeats, he tells us,

> makes his system for the poet and hero, and begins by predicating their defeat. Beyond Promethean quest, for him, there is only the cyclic renewal of quest, and the renewed necessity for heroic defeat. *A Vision* exists to pattern the drama of defeat.[41]

What is strange here is that Bloom recognises so many aspects of *A Vision* which are intelligible as aspects of tragic vision, but then dismisses them. He acknowledges that 'The *antithetical* quester must be content to exhaust himself in a struggle with his destiny, in the knowledge that he can never win, that his fate must be his only freedom.'[42] He argues that phase seventeen shows those who 'have Yeats's version of the tragic sense of life, for one must lose the woman one loves, confronted always as one is by a recalcitrant Muse'.[43] But, where Whitaker comments on the dangers of a course seeking 'completeness' rather than 'perfection',[44] Bloom sees Yeats as choosing sublimity rather than truth: 'The *antithetical* quest is for beauty, and then through beauty not to truth but to the soul's own sublimity, its heightened sense of itself.'[45] Bloom concludes here with an astonishing assertion:

> Yeats courageously insisted that we begin to live when we conceive of life as tragedy, but his own life and poetic career indicate that we cease to live when we can no longer conceive a possible sublimity for ourselves, and for Yeats tragedy was not sublime enough.[46]

To make sense of this we have to recognise that, for Bloom, tragedy and apocalypse are incompatible, as he tells us Blake insisted, and that '*A Vision* is Blakean enough to be uncomfortable with any tragic definitions of the highest art'.[47]

What is an apocalypse? Is it compatible with tragedy? We have seen Whitaker define *A Vision* as apocalyptic, wholeness transcending difference. Bloom defines *A Vision* as 'technically an apocalypse', because it 'does try to pass a Last Judgement on its own age and its own poet'.[48] He insists that 'the purpose of an apocalypse is to reveal truth, and so help stimulate a restoration of men to an unfallen state'.[49] Denis Donoghue sees apocalypse and tragic form as related elements in *A Vision*: 'One of the purposes of *A Vision* is to declare the susceptibility of time and history to tragic pattern, Nietzschean in tone: the past becomes a memory theatre, apocalyptic in its climax.'[50]

In its broadest definition there is no reason why apocalypse should be incompatible with tragic vision. Since 'apocalypse' means vision or revelation, nothing precludes that such vision be tragic. However, apocalypse has attracted to itself a wide range of associations which may be summed up as including prophetic vision which heralds the end of the world or an order. It can also imply judgement – the final judgement, since vision may reveal ultimate truth. This element of judgement associates apocalypse with a purgative and cleansing role and can therefore imply a restoration of man, through the refining fire, to his original unity and innocence. Apocalypse is therefore associated with the idea of a fall from grace and a passionate appeal for a return with an assumption that this will follow on revelation. A tragic apocalypse, however, may be seen as a revelation of fall. Its sense of an ultimate return to grace is severely curtailed. For the tragic writer that return may only be achieved momentarily and in the tragic moment itself. The tragic revelation is bleak:

> Our fires, our sacrifices, and our prayers
> The gods abominate. How should the birds
> Give any other than ill-omened voices,
> Gorged with the dregs of blood that man has shed?

A tragic apocalypse has nothing to do with a restoration of man to grace. In Yeats, apocalypse or final judgement is to be arrived at at every moment, as Yeats suggests in his writing on Synge (see *E&I*, p. 339) or in 'Vacillation':

> Test every work of intellect or faith,
> And everything that your own hands have wrought,
> And call those works extravagance of breath
> That are not suited for such men as come
> Proud, open-eyed and laughing to the tomb.
> (*CP*, p. 283)

It is perhaps on this issue that Yeats and his Romantic ancestors part company. Remarks from another essay of Harold Bloom's, on *The Four Zoas*, throw some light on the problem. Bloom draws our attention to Enion's lament:

> What is the price of Experience? do men buy it for
>   a song?
> Or wisdom for a dance in the street? No, it is bought
>   with the price
> Of all that a man hath, his house, his wife, his children.
> Wisdom is sold in the desolate market where none come
>   to buy,
> And in the wither'd field where the farmer plows for
>   bread in vain.[52]

This is close to the desolate landscape of the dance plays explored in the last chapter, but the choice Yeats makes in such a situation is very different from Blake's. Harold Bloom remarks that 'The burden of Enion's song is a thought that . . . can lead only to madness or apocalypse, for the song is a culminating lament for lost innocence, organised about the idea that human pleasure is based on a wilful ignorance concerning the suffering of others'.[53] Enion's lament reveals how different is Yeats's vision, for it does not suggest any alternative or enlightenment of a social nature. Such an alternative is seen in 'Nineteen Hundred and Nineteen' (*CP*, pp. 232–7), for example, as illusory:

> O what fine thought we had because we thought
> That the worst rogues and rascals had died out. . . .
> Now days are dragon-ridden . . . .

The vision Yeats reveals is one where 'The night can sweat with terror' and a universe in which

> All men are dancers and their tread
> Goes to the barbarous clamour of a gong.

Tragedy could not exist in a world in which solutions were possible. It is, I believe, with tragedy as much as with Yeats's cyclical system that Bloom argues.

In *The Death of Tragedy* George Steiner stresses the need for a pessimistic vision in tragedy. He argues that Romanticism was predominantly optimistic and linked to the revolutionary:

> In romanticism there is the liberation of thought from the deductive sobriety of Cartesian and Newtonian rationalism. . . . There is, both intuitively and practically, a liberation of the individual from pre-determined hierarchies of social station and caste.[54]

Harold Bloom, as we have seen, shows Blake in rebellion from 'an inadequate version of reason and an unjust organization of society'.[55] Steiner argues that at the heart of the Romantic liberation lay a belief in the perfectibility of human nature. With this comes a diminution of responsibility:

> Responsibility lay with schooling or environment, for evil cannot be native to the soul and because the individual is not wholly responsible, he cannot be wholly damned . . . . The crime leads not to punishment but to redemption.[56]

This is a highly simplified treatment of Romanticism. No one could accuse Blake of avoiding responsibility. But this does throw light on two very different definitions of apocalypse. Apocalypse is seen by a critic such as Bloom as a force which not only can, but should, 'fallen, fallen light renew'.[57] He rejects the idea of an apocalypse which may reveal, as Jan Kott remarks, the stage of history littered with fresh corpses.[58] Steiner's remarks on perfectibility and pessimism draw us to Yeats's interest in Castiglione's *The Book of the Courtier* and Nietzsche's writings, which are both concerned with these themes.

Nietzsche Yeats discovered in 1902, Castiglione, suggests Corinna Salvadori, in 1903.[59] Both help Yeats define his concept of the hero. Briefly, the courtier or Castiglionian element of the hero defines him as an educated accomplished man, 'Soldier, scholar, horseman, he' (*CP*, p. 149), the epitome of the cultured, disciplined, civilised and many-sided. The Nietzschean hero, while marked also by discipline and, ultimately, gaiety is closely related to the figure of the scapegoat or sacrificial god-substitute. The Nietzschean hero confronts the dark, is at war. The Castiglionian hero is in pursuit of elegance and grace. He too faces war, but with grace, with style.

Corinna Salvadori defines Castiglione's world as that of the humanist. She quotes from Pico della Mirandola on the possibilities open to the Renaissance man:

> We have made thee neither of heaven nor of earth, neither mortal nor immortal so that with freedom of choice and with honour, as though the maker and moulder of thyself thou mayest fashion thyself in whatever shape thou shalt prefer . . . . Thou shalt have the power out of thy soul's judgement to be reborn in the higher forms, which are divine.[60]

She sums up the humanist philosophy:

> The humanists saw man's personality as something rich and complex which contained the properties of all beings; it was a harmonious fusion of body and senses, of heart and intelligence endowed with the power to attain perfection through self-improvement, to transcend the physical and reach divine contemplation.[61]

One can see this search for perfection and transcendence as characteristic of Yeats's subjective man in search of the fifteenth phase. Salvadori argues that 'Castiglione was not writing a manual of education for the courtier – ideal though he should be – but his subject was man, man in his quest for perfection.'[62] She sees the motivation for this pursuit as Love:

> The fundamental force that spurs on our ideal courtier is love – love from its lowest state which is the contemplation of physical beauty to its utmost perfection which is union with God. The spiritual formation and self-perfection of the courtier must be such that they will lead him to a final ecstasy comparable to that of a St. Paul or a St. Francis.[63]

This is close to much of Yeats's early poetry, particularly that moulded by Rosicrucianism, but remains a constant element throughout Yeats's poetry. In 'Among School Children', for example, as in the later 'Vacillation', Yeats responds to the miraculous and sweet-smelling power of Love: the nuns who worship its image, 'The body of Saint Teresa . . . undecayed in tomb' (*CP*, p. 285). The courtier is above all the advocate of choice, self-definition and responsibility. As regards the motive, love, we must note the identification of physical and spiritual beauty and recall Yeats's frequent references to Dante's 'Unity of Being', 'the perfectly proportioned human body' (*V*, p. 82). Love is central to *A Vision* as symbol of the solved antinomy, as love which would not change that which it loves (p. 275). But such love also unleashes a world of suffering, of frustrated desire, of the man who accepts loss while still yearning for what he desires.

The other side of the courtier's choice is chance, what Yeats in *A Vision* terms fate rather than destiny. The beloved may lure, cheat, destroy, annihilate. The universe too is hostile. The Nietzschean universe is full of chance. One can imagine that a Yeats, reading Castiglione, would find in Nietzsche the Dionysian terror with which to confront and balance the Apollonian ideal of Castiglione's courtier. Nietzsche defines the world as conflict. He nowhere speaks of perfection. Love too is seen as conflict, 'just as procreation depends on the duality of the sexes, involving perpetual strife with only periodically intervening reconciliations'.[64] The courtier is individual, controlled, particular. Nietzsche confronts him with the common, the undifferentiated mob, with loss of control.

In *The Birth of Tragedy* Nietzsche defines a contrast between imagist and rhythmical art. The Apollonian is concerned with shape, form, ideal and beauty, the Dionysian with eternal rhythm, destructive of the individual. Nietzsche quotes from Schopenhauer to define the position of Apollonian man:

> Just as in a stormy sea that, unbounded in all directions, raises and drops mountainous waves, howling, a sailor sits in a boat and trusts in his frail bark: so in the midst of a world of torments the individual human being sits quietly supported by and trusting in the *principium individuationis*.[65]

Nietzsche sees tragedy as an ideal balance between these two forces, in which the Dionysian abyss or howling ocean becomes mirrored in the individual. Nietzsche's definition of the Dionysian abyss, or stormy sea without, is enlightening in relation to Yeats's treatments of anarchy, violence and the Vision of Evil. For Nietzsche draws our attention not only to the Dionysian in its ideal balance in Greek tragedy. He turns also to the Dionysian barbarian:

> From all quarters of the ancient world – to say nothing here of the modern – . . . we can point to the existence of Dionysian festivals, types which bear, at best, the same relation to the Greek festivals which the bearded satyr, who borrowed his name and attributes from the goat, bears to Dionysius himself. In nearly every case these festivals centred in extravagant sexual licentiousness, whose waves overwhelmed all family life and its venerable traditions; the most savage natural instincts were unleashed, including even that horrible mixture of sensuality and cruelty which has always seemed to me to be the real 'witches' brew'.[66]

We meet this in Blake's 'The Mental Traveller',[67] later in Yeats's *The Resurrection* and in its strongest form in *Purgatory*.

Nietzsche's 'mystery doctrine of tragedy' – described as 'the fundamental knowledge of the oneness of everything existent, the conception of individuation as the primal cause of evil, and of art as the joyous hope that the spell of individuation may be broken in augury of a restored oneness'[68] – insists on a vision of an eternal life which accepts the destruction of the individual. Its emphasis is on the primal and primordial, just as Yeats emphasises the Great Mind and Memory of nature in his essay on magic (*E&I*, p. 28), and the Daimonic Memory in *A Vision*. It is a vision based on reverence for myth as a vehicle for truth, rather than linear history, progress, optimism and science. In tragedy, argues Nietzsche,

> We are to recognise that all that comes into being must be ready for a sorrowful end; we are forced to look into the terrors of the individual existence – yet we are not to become rigid with fear: a metaphysical comfort tears us momentarily from the bustle of the changing figures. We are really for a brief moment primordial being itself, feeling its raging desire for existence and joy in existence; the struggle, the pain, the destruction of phenomena, now appear as necessary to us, in view of the excess of countless forms of existence which force and pull one another into life, in view of the exuberant fertility of the universal will.[69]

A measure of comfort, then, lies in the recognition of the under-lying and eternal fertility and energy of life itself.

The death of tragedy, on the other hand, depends, in Nietz-sche's view, on an optimistic view, a belief in knowledge rather than wisdom which finds its first expression in Socrates. It is the modern disease. Nietzsche sees these forces – Apollonian, Dio-nysian and Socratic – as methods of survival, each in its way illusory.

In 'An Attempt at Self-Criticism' Nietzsche makes some modifications to his original thesis and further examines the significance of tragedy and the concept of tragic joy. He begins with a glance at the Golden Age: 'The best turned out, most beautiful, most envied type of humanity to date, those most apt to seduce us to life, the Greeks – how now? They of all people should have *needed* tragedy?'[70] He suggests that pessimism may be a sign of health, optimism of decline, a clutching at straws, protection from a truth too awful to bear:

> Is there a pessimism of *strength*? An intellectual predilection for the hard, gruesome, evil, problematic aspect of existence, prompted by the well-being, by over-flowing health, by the

-fullness of existence? Is it perhaps possible to suffer precisely from overfullness? The sharp-eyed courage that tempts and attempts, that *craves* the frightful as enemy, the worthy enemy, against whom one can test one's strength? From whom one learns what it means 'to be frightened'?[71]

With Nietzsche, as with Yeats, there is no room for the weak, no pity in the accustomed sense of the term. The emphasis is on power, will, mastery, courage, conflict and energy. Both Nietzsche and Yeats see their contemporary worlds as degenerate and in need of the pessimistic vision in order to survive.

What lies at the end of this tragic vision? Stoic resignation? Joy? Some 'metaphysical comfort'? The 'fundamental knowledge of the oneness of everything?' Nietzsche in 'An Attempt at Self-Criticism' reflects on his conclusions in *The Birth of Tragedy*, questioning their validity. Tragedy, he argues emphatically, has nothing to do with 'resignation' as Schopenhauer had suggested.[72] He seeks to replace 'the art of metaphysical comfort' with '*this-worldly* comfort first': 'you ought to begin to laugh, my young friends, if you are hell-bent on remaining pessimists.'[73] The concept of tragic joy, then, is hard to define. It veers from label to label, from gesture to gesture, from 'resignation' to 'acceptance', gaiety, joy, ecstasy and, finally, laughter, which in Yeats becomes 'the brazen winged beast . . . [of] laughing, ecstatic destruction' (*VPl*, p. 932), energy itself. The rejection of 'resignation' and the attempt to define an 'acceptance' of individual destruction which is yet an active participation is important in Yeats's definition of the hero's tragic joy. It makes all the difference between a Vision of Evil, the poet's triumphant enactment of loss and desire, and the idea of art as mere substitution of ideal for experience.

Nietzsche's definition of the tragic hero and his stress on affirmation, self-definition and a hero laughing in the face of death and destruction are seen by Denis Donoghue as being absorbed almost without dilution by Yeats. He draws attention to *The Will to Power*:

It is not the satisfaction of the will that causes pleasure . . . but rather the will's forward thrust and again and again becoming master over that which stands in its way. . . . [Pleasure] lies precisely in the dissatisfaction of the will, in the fact that the

will is never satisfied unless it has opponents and resist-
ances . . .[74]

Donoghue comments, 'One of the distinctive qualities of Yeats's
imagination is that it revels in combat; cultivates at the risk of
aggression, power at the risk of violence lest the organism die of
sloth and satisfaction.'[75]

II

In *A Vision* Yeats describes twenty-eight phases of the moon's
cycle and their relationship to the individual psyche and to the
historical cycle. In these phases Yeats attempts to hold together
the whole range of human and supernatural possibility. The first
and fifteenth are, I should argue, of greatest importance. The
first phase stands at the centre of what Yeats terms the primary
or objective, the fifteenth at the centre of the antithetical or
subjective. The primary is passive, the subjective creative. These
are absolute states which can never be fully incarnated by man,
but man is torn between the two extremes. In phase one the
moon is entirely dark and man is totally without direction or
responsibility. It is a phase of terror and associated in Yeats's
poetry with ugliness, mob frenzy and loss of individual identity.
It is crucial in terms of the historical cycle. Yeats sees this as the
moment in history when the thirteenth cone, the unique, in-
tervenes, when a new historical order is annunciated. The annunciation may herald a primary era (as with Mary) or an
antithetical (as with Leda), but it always heralds a meeting
between man and god, and it also presages, as we shall see, that
the cycle will be tragic, that the meeting between man and god
will unleash a story of division and conflict. For the individual
the first phase is a nightmare in which all beauty, form and the
particular and individual are destroyed by the monstrous and
undifferentiated. It is analogous to what Yeats terms the Vision
of Evil. The fifteenth phase, on the other hand, is a phase of
ecstasy, Unity of Being, joy and delight. At the first phase there
is uniformity rather than unity. The fifteenth phase is achieved
consciously, dramatically. The first phase is its necessary counter-
point, intimating ultimate defeat and the return of the cycle.
Taken together these two poles represent desire and dread,

terror and delight, harmony or Unity of Being and discord or the Vision of Evil. For Yeats tragic joy, or tragic vision, is compounded of tension between these two forces.

The poem 'The Double Vision of Michael Robartes' (*CP*, pp. 192–4)[76] explains and defines these two phases. Its title indicates how both phases are necessary to vision, to the double vision of tragedy. The poem is divided into three sections. In the first, Yeats's *persona* summons 'to the mind's eye' the first phase of the moon's cycle:

> Under blank eyes and fingers never still
> The particular is pounded till it is man.
> When had I my own will?
> O not since life began.
>
> Constrained, arraigned, baffled, bent and unbent
> By these wire-jointed jaws and limbs of wood,
> Themselves obedient,
> Knowing not evil and good . . . .

Though without powers of judgement or will, man in this phase is obedient. His obedience implies the existence of some force of power outside himself. Figures who recall those of 'The Magi' are above, uncaring and indifferent:

> They do not even feel, so abstract are they,
> So dead beyond our death,
> Triumph that we obey.

But underneath lies a sense of impending creation – 'The particular is pounded'; we feel 'some hidden magical breath'. We are prepared for the next section of the poem, the fifteenth phase.

In this section, two poles are held in balance, the Sphinx and the Buddha. The images are concrete:

> Although I saw it all in the mind's eye
> There can be nothing solider till I die;
> I saw it all by the moon's light
> Now at its fifteenth night.

In this phase intellect and love are balanced:

> One lashed her tail; her eyes lit by the moon
> Gazed upon all things known, all things un-
>   known,
> In triumph of intellect
> With motionless head erect.
>
> That other's moonlit eye-balls never moved,
> Being fixed on all things loved, all things unloved,
> Yet little peace he had
> For those that love are sad.

Neither is dominant and the two forces of reason and nature are arrested. This phase introduces Yeats's *persona* to harmony, Unity of Being, here shown in the image of the dancing girl. She, like the Sphinx and the Buddha, is uncaring, indifferent, caught up in the contemplation of herself. She becomes the dance which she performs:

> O little did they care who danced between,
> And little she by whom her dance was seen
> So she had out-distanced thought.
> Body perfection brought,
>
> For what but eye and ear silence the mind
> With the minute particulars of mankind?
> Mind moved yet seemed to stop
> As 'twere a spinning-top.

The third section returns us to the poet. Whereas the Sphinx and Buddha framing the central vision of beauty and unity are caught in an eternal moment –

> In contemplation had those three so wrought
> Upon a moment and so stretched it out
> That they, time overthrown,
> Were dead yet flesh and bone

– the poet remains trapped in the whirling movement of the gyres:

> To such a pitch of folly I am brought,
> Being caught between the pull
> Of the dark moon and the full . . . .

The lines echo the first section of the poem – 'When had I my own will?' – but the poet has been rewarded with a vision of unity. Yeats tells us in *A Vision*, 'Life is an endeavour made vain by the four sails of its mill, to come to a double contemplation, that of the chosen Image, that of the fated Image' (p. 94). Here the poet contemplates the desired image of joy and beauty against the image of chaos and deformity which is fated to return. He ends by celebrating his glimpse of unity in the midst of the recognition of his own loss:

> Thereon I made my moan,
> And after kissed a stone,
>
> And after that arranged it in a song
> Seeing that I, ignorant for so long,
> Had been rewarded thus
> In Cormac's ruined house.

This is a poem about creation and poetry. Creation grows out of conflict and opposition and the poet is rewarded with a vision of unity and beauty. In this way the poem is an expression of tragic joy, the momentary achievement of style against a world of chaos. The song captures the timeless moment of joy.

It should be noted that Yeats presents the fifteenth phase as a paradox. Movement appears as stillness, death is flesh and bone. In 'The Phases of the Moon' (*CP*, pp. 183–8), too, we are shown this phase as a paradox in which soul becomes body and thought image. All is made tangible and particular and yet certain divisions remain. There is still separation. Beholder is distinct from beheld. Helen Vendler comments on the central paradox of this phase, in which unity does not preclude separation. She finds an answer in the poem 'Solomon and the Witch' (*CP*, pp. 199–200),[77] in which the crowing of the cockerel seems to indicate that chance and choice are one, that

> All that the brigand apple brought
> And this foul world were dead at last.

But this is thwarted. The dream of a love in which two lovers, 'Though several, are a single light' fails. The poem ends, nevertheless, with an affirmation: 'O! Solomon! let us try again.' Vendler therefore argues,

> If the perfect congruence between imagination and reality were to occur, and the world were to end, love would cease to exist – and for Yeats, that is an unthinkable conclusion. The notion of love implies two separate persons, and if Solomon and Sheba were not distinct, the dialogue, and therefore the poem, would be impossible.[78]

It is for this reason, she argues, that Yeats tells us,

> Now contemplation and desire, united into one, inhabit a world where every beloved image has bodily form, and every bodily form is loved. This love knows nothing of desire, for desire implies effort, and though there is still separation from the loved object, love accepts the separation as necessary to its own existence.   (*V*, p. 136)[79]

Vendler concludes, 'The poet, then, tries endlessly for the perfect fusion of reality and image, but at the same time sees their individual recalcitrance as the condition for creation and so accepts it.'[80] Another way of looking at the paradoxical nature of this phase is to see it as a differentiation between uniformity and unity. For it is possible, I feel, that two lights, though several, may be one, as in the poem 'Ribh at the Tomb of Baile and Aillin':

> when such bodies join
> There is no touching here, nor touching there,
> Nor straining joy, but whole is joined to whole;
> For the intercourse of angels is a light
> Where for its moment both seem lost, consumed.
> (*CP*, p. 327)

Yet it must be stressed that the light, the moment of joy, lasts but 'for its moment' and, caught between two poles, we are allowed only a glimpse of delight.

III

In reading *A Vision* as a tragic apocalypse Yeats's treatment of history is of paramount importance. *A Vision* has three major historical cycles in mind – that announced to Leda, that to Mary, and the new one which he prophesies as imminent. Yeats begins *A Vision* by announcing 'a new divinity' (p. 27). But this divinity is not our redeemer in any conventional sense. Yeats sees the two past cycles represented by Oedipus and Christ as 'the two scales of a balance' (p. 29) between which civilisation veers. Yeats warns us that the Christian era may have 'burned to the socket', but there is no suggestion that the new age is not similarly fated:

> After an age of necessity, truth, goodness, mechanism, science, democracy, abstraction, peace, comes an age of freedom, fiction, evil, kindred, art, aristocracy, particularity, war. . . . Love war because of its horror, that belief be changed, civilisation renewed.   (pp. 52–3)

History veers between two poles of what may be called intellect and nature, Asia and Europe, Oedipus and Christ. In *A Vision* Yeats makes use of Hegel to define the perpetual swing from one to the other: 'Hegel identifies Asia with Nature; he sees the whole process of civilisation as an escape from Nature; partly achieved by Greece, fully achieved by Christianity' (p. 202).

In an introduction to *The Holy Mountain* Yeats examines Hegel more closely. Hegel believes in progress. Since Oedipus solved the riddle of the Sphinx, 'intellect or Spirit, that which has value in itself, began to prevail and now in Hegel's own day the climax had come, not crippled age but wisdom. . . . God's will proved to be man's will' (*E&I*, p. 467). In other words, for Hegel, man might be said to have both knowledge and power (this pair forming yet another Yeatsian antinomy), if we take power to come from nature, which man is now seen to control. Yeats puts a reply to and rejection of this optimistic philosophy in the mouth of an imagined Balzac:

> Man's intellect or Spirit can do nothing but bear witness; Nature alone is active. . . . I refuse to confine Nature to claw, paw, and hoof. It is the irrational glory that reaches perfection

at the mid-moment, at the Renaissance of every civilisation.
(Ibid.)

Yeats accepts Hegel's dialectic but with reservations. He transforms it into a cyclical movement. Europe and Asia form an
antinomy and Yeats often refers to them as 'symbolic' (*V*,
p. 205). Every civilisation grows out of this antinomy. In *A Vision*
Yeats rejects the idea of progress emphatically. While the his-
torian sees history as continual advancement – of Greece over
Persia, of Rome over Greece, of the agricultural age over the
hunter's – Yeats insists that 'all civilisations [are] equal at their
best; every phase returns, therefore, in some sense every civilisation' (p. 206). For Yeats there is no linear progression: 'Each age
unwinds the thread another age has wound' (ibid.). Yeats identifies these cycles explicitly with tragedy. History itself is personified as a tragic personage who

> must display an almost superhuman will or the cry will not
> touch our sympathy. The loss of control over thought comes
> towards the end; first a sinking in upon the moral being, then
> the last surrender, the irrational cry, revelation – the scream
> of Juno's peacock.   (p. 268)

Yeats clearly sees his age as being at the end of a cycle, the
primary cycle dominated by Christianity. His reaction to the
imminent change veers between horror at catastrophe and delight at change. But the new era can only be imagined in relation
to the two past eras the poet is imaginatively aware of – more
specifically, the two past annunciations, made to Leda and
Mary. In *The Lonely Tower* T. R. Henn comments,

> Two Annunciations form a pattern in history: Leda and the
> Virgin. . . . Both events concern the union of god-head and
> woman. Both produce momentous births. The eggs of Leda
> give rise to the fall of Troy. . . . The outcome of the union is
> further history or myth, pagan or Christian, Love and war.
> But what of the woman? Yeats speculates continually on the
> emotion of woman in such a crisis. Did Leda or Mary by that
> act become half or wholly divine?[81]

This parallels the transformation which overcomes the Guardian
in *At the Hawk's Well*:

It was her mouth, and yet not she, that cried.
It was that shadow cried behind her mouth . . . .
                                        (*CPl*, p. 215)

Helen Vendler asks here 'what knowledge remains in the mind
as the residue of possession by the Daimon?'[82] But what differentiates the meeting of man and Daimon at the fifteenth phase
from the meeting of man with the thirteenth cone at the turn of
the cycle is that in the first encounter the meeting is the achievement of deliberate conscious activity on the part of the individual
to find his Mask or Image. In the second encounter man is
engulfed and overwhelmed. Such an encounter, despite its ca-
lamitous consequences, may be welcomed as a meeting between
man and divinity and a momentary achievement of unity. But in
A Vision Yeats stresses what happens in 'human experience',
stresses that 'all things fall into a series of antinomies' (p. 193).
Knowledge and power, intellect and Nature will be separated.
We can only speculate on what happens at the moment of
annunciation: 'Did she put on his knowledge with his power?'
(*CP*, p. 241). Yeats stresses that annunciation is also the literal
birth of tragedy. We cannot escape more than momentarily from
the whirlpool of his universe. Each annunciation heralds a new
cycle of tragedy.

In a note on 'The Second Coming' (*CP*, pp. 210–11) Yeats
draws our attention to the imminence of a catastrophe that is
also a reversal:

All our scientific, democratic, fact-accumulating, hetero-
geneous civilisation belongs to the outward gyre and prepares
not the continuance of itself but the revelation as in a lightning
flash, . . . that will not strike only in one place . . . of the
civilisation that must slowly take its place.[83]

The poem has to be seen in relation to such poems as 'A Prayer
for my Daughter' and 'Nineteen Hundred and Nineteen', which,
while accepting the necessary pattern of history, expose its
destructive violence. Jon Stallworthy in *Between the Lines* shows
how the poem grew out of a despondency at the First World
War, the German invasion of Russia, the collapse and murder of
the Russian royal family. Early drafts contain also a reference to
Burke. Yeats's apocalyptic prophecy is rooted in contemporary
events, but as the poem is developed and revised:

Already German and Russian, Burke and Pitt, mob and murderer, and the judge before his dock have fallen away. The poem's scope and focus have widened. Lest particular details distract the reader's eye and limit his vision, Yeats introduces more general terms, such as 'anarchy', 'the ceremony of innocence', 'the good', and 'the worst'.[84]

As the poem opens, the mob rules, anarchy prevails. The predominant emotion is horror and terror. The turning of the gyre spirals into the flight of the falcon:

> Turning and turning in the widening gyre
> The falcon cannot hear the falconer;
> Things fall apart; the centre cannot hold;
> Mere anarchy is loosed upon the world,
> The blood-dimmed tide is loosed, and everywhere
> The ceremony of innocence is drowned;
> The best lack all conviction, while the worst
> Are full of passionate intensity.

This horrifying and destructive vision builds up a momentum of hysterical excitement and ends almost with a plea:

> Surely some revelation is at hand;
> Surely the Second Coming is at hand.

Yeats's plea is for some kind of redemption. The poem shows how limited is the redemption possible in his system. It is not permanent but a renewal. Yeats seeks some image which may explain or make tangible the revelation he senses and calls for.

So, in The Second Coming', the landscape is deliberately vague, the apparition shadowy:

> somewhere in sands of the desert
> A shape with lion body and the head of a man,
> A gaze blank and pitiless as the sun,
> Is moving its slow thighs, while all about it
> Reel shadows of the indignant desert birds.

But the new annunciation does not herald any ultimate freedom. Everything about it is harsh and discordant, its gaze 'blank and pitiless'. The poet turns to the previous annunciation, Christ's, to reveal how every annunciation unwinds a relentless thread of conflict:

> but now I know
> That twenty centuries of stony sleep
> Were vexed to nightmare by a rocking cradle . . . .

The movement of the cradle echoes the turning of the gyre. The cradled child becomes a harbinger of conflict and nightmare. The poem ends on a grotesque and threatening note:

> And what rough beast, its hour come
>   round at last,
> Slouches towards Bethlehem to be born?

Yeats is far more intimately concerned with the myth of Leda than with the annunciation made to Mary. He cannot see Christ as the Messiah, but only as a Messiah. He sees Judaism as a rigid system, whereas the system Yeats seeks to create is constantly changing and reversing. Christianity provides an ultimate redemption, salvation. Yeats's system does not. For Yeats the myth of Leda generates or gives birth to the Greek tragic cycle. But it is not merely that Yeats sees Leda as the literal mother of Helen and Clytemnestra. The rape of Leda by the swan contains in itself the birth of tragedy. 'Leda and the Swan' (*CP*, p. 241) is a revelation in the same sense as in 'The Cold Heaven' – sudden and total. Mary in 'The Mother of God'[85] is chosen, not choosing: Leda is raped. In the first four lines of the octet Yeats concentrates on the extraordinary conjunction of bird and woman:

> A sudden blow: the great wings beating still
> Above the staggering girl, her thighs caressed
> By the dark webs, her nape caught in his bill,
> He holds her helpless breast upon his breast.

Leda is 'helpless', 'staggering'. The second four lines of the octet focus on her response:

> How can those terrified vague fingers push
> The feathered glory from her loosening thighs?

She is overwhelmed. In a sense she does become the bird, does
become divine:

> And how can body, laid in that white rush,
> But feel the strange heart beating where it
>   lies?

She takes on his power.

The first part of the sestet focuses on the tragic cycle which the
rape unleashes. The very act of imparting divine power and
knowledge to the mortal engenders tragedy:

> A shudder in the loins engenders there
> The broken wall, the burning roof and tower
> And Agamemnon dead.

It seems that in the moment of impact both knowledge and
power can be combined. Leda, helpless and innocent, becomes a
vessel containing both, but only with tragic consequences. The
swan dominates, is absolute master:

> > Being so caught up,
> So mastered by the brute blood of the air,
> Did she put on his knowledge with his power
> Before the indifferent beak could let her drop?

Helen Vendler focuses her attention on Leda's response. She
argues that Leda,

> although she attempts a helpless resistance, finally is stirred
> by the presence of the 'feathered glory', and the shudder in the
> loins is hers as well as the swan's. We sense this, I think, in
> Yeats's language; Leda's thighs are 'loosening' not 'loosen'ed';
> she may be terrified, but she finds the swan glorious . . . she is
> not numbed, but alive to the strange heart-beat. The power,
> then, although in itself Olympian and 'indifferent', is some-
> thing that can move the heart as well as master the body. Leda
> in the octave is 'caught', but in the sestet she is 'caught up';
> there lies all the difference between captivity and rapture.[86]

Helen Vendler sees the last three lines of the sestet as the poem's
central issue. She reads the poem in terms of the poet. The poem

asks, 'is the momentary ecstatic cooperation in the assault continued beyond the climactic moment into a new knowledge?'[87] That new knowledge, it seems to me, is implanted by the bird's powerful assault and it includes a tragic knowledge, 'A shudder in the loins', which relates the act of love to tragic destruction. Vendler argues that 'the central concern of the poem is not, as Ellmann says, "whether power and knowledge can ever be united in life", but rather whether a special knowledge attaches to the conferred power of artistic creation'.[88] I think that the poem does contain a reflection on inspiration and on poetic creation, but the flaw in Helen Vendler's argument seems to me that she overlooks the implications of the first three lines of the sestet, the question of the potential outcome of such revelation. Whether seen in terms of the poet or in terms of the historical cycles of *A Vision*, the outcome of revelation is perceived to be a recognition of tragedy, conflict and catastrophe.

Perhaps the most significant if least tangible contribution which the system of *A Vision* makes towards an understanding of Yeats's tragic vision is its capacity to help Yeats evoke an atmosphere. It provides him with a kind of symbolic shorthand. Reading a poem we are aware of a recognisable state of being, which corresponds almost to a sense of place. A reference to the moon, or to a moonless night, a reference to forms of beauty, or to the deformed and ugly, gives us an immediate sense of arrival at a familiar if often frightening area of experience. This is particularly the case in the poem 'I See Phantoms of Hatred and of the Heart's Fullness and of the Coming Emptiness' (*CP*, pp. 231–2). In this poem we see Yeats's system in use as a fulcrum which balances diverse Yeatsian preoccupations: the individual plight in the historical cycle, the mob in relation to the isolated individual, Ireland as a scene of tragic conflict, the two poles of Unity of Being and the Vision of Evil. The poem is an anatomy of the double vision of tragedy, with its central moment of beauty, order and delight towards which we strive. This is surrounded by the sense of imminent catastrophe, the returning cycle of horror, deformity and collapse.

The poem opens on the summit of a tower, which is itself the poem's eye or centre. From this vantage-point an eerie landscape is described, strange, frightening, scoured by mist and snow:

> A mist that is like blown snow is sweeping over all;
> Valley, river, and elms, under the light of a moon

> That seems unlike itself, that seems unchangeable,
> A glittering sword out of the east.

Without having to explain his images in the terminology of *A Vision*, Yeats here presents an emblem of the full moon, of the fifteenth phase which the poet holds against the chaos of the first phase. The 'glittering sword' remains as an emblem of the full moon throughout the poem. The stormy atmosphere of wind and mist creates an ambiguity which allows Yeats to move from chaos to unity, as if detecting patterns of order and chaos in the random movements of the clouds. Now in the first stanza, the moon's light is blotted out: 'A puff of wind / And those white glimmering fragments of the mist sweep by.' Terror is unloosed. The emphasis is on fragmentation. From the opening lines, which evoke a particular landscape, Yeats moves on to build up a sense of engulfing chaos in which the outer tumult is mirrored in the inner mind,

> Frenzies bewilder, reveries perturb the mind;
> Monstrous familiar images swim to the mind's eye.

We approach the first phase of the moon; tossed to and fro, we are caught in a senseless tumult. Yeats's notes on the poem explain Jaques Molay, a fourteenth-century Templar (*CP*, p. 534). Yeats writes, 'A cry for vengeance . . . seems to me fit symbol for those who labour from hatred, and so for sterility in various kinds' (ibid.). This recalls Yeats's comments on 'The Dolls' and 'The Magi'; nor can it be divorced from an Irish context. Part of the Irish heritage Yeats sees as hatred: 'the political class in Ireland . . . have suffered through the cultivation of hatred as the one energy of their movement, a deprivation which is the intellectual equivalent of a certain surgical operation' (*A*, p. 486). The poem is set in civil war, in a time of uncertainty, but Yeats, it seems to me, takes the theme to embrace loss of control, the self-control which holds a civilisation together. As in 'The Second Coming', Yeats transforms the particular into the universal. Hatred, sterility and wanton destruction dominate. Yeats concentrates on the horror of the turning wheel of history:

> In cloud-pale rags, or in lace,
> The rage-driven, rage-tormented, and rage-hungry
> troop,

Trooper belabouring trooper, biting at arms or at face,
Plunges towards nothing . . . .

The horrifying world encountered here is Yeats's Vision of Evil
and illustrates what Whitaker means when he talks of Yeats's
interior Lucifer. In this poem Yeats's *persona* is almost swept
away by self-devouring rage:

> and I, my wits astray
> Because of all that senseless tumult, all but cried
> For vengeance on the murderers of Jaques Molay.

Yeats turns from external anarchy, the tragic circumstances of
life in which we are caught, to the individual dilemma. Yeats's
persona here is like the man of phase seventeen in *A Vision*: his
self-control is 'falling asunder'. He is like a bursting pod and his
aim is to hide 'this separation and disorder' (p. 141) from himself
and others. The poet's weapon is his Mask, his style. In the
poem, then, the poet uses these as his weapons against both an
outer and an inner chaos.

The third stanza moves directly out of rage to ecstasy, design
and order. The image of the 'glittering sword' surfaces again in
the radiant description of unity which follows. The images Yeats
now evokes are sensuous and concrete in contrast to the self-
devouring images which come before:

> Their legs long, delicate and slender, aquamarine their
>   eyes,
> Magical unicorns bear ladies on their backs.

These mythical beasts, with eyes as blue as water, form a
haunting contrast to the angry mob. The ladies are untroubled
and at peace. The image of water is carried through:

> their minds are but a pool
> Where even longing drowns under its own excess;
> Nothing but stillness can remain when hearts are full
> Of their own sweetness, bodies of their loveliness.

This is the fifteenth phase, where 'All thought becomes an image
and the soul / Becomes a body', concrete and self-absorbed.

Whitaker sees these ladies as decadent and comments, 'However beautiful, it is the deathly goal of Narcissus.'[89] He argues that they show the fifteenth phase transformed from 'an abounding jet of life', as in 'Ancestral Houses', into an 'eternal stillness of self-contemplation'.[90] He argues that, 'For the living speaker these ladies and unicorns can image not a solution but one term of a predicament'.[91] He argues that the poet who does not yield to the mob 'cannot now adopt the transcendent narcissism of aquamarine or closed eyes': 'The poem renders a precarious solution: not the imagined escape from the prison of self through freedom in love, but the open-eyed self-recognition of the half-trapped poet.'[92]

I cannot altogether accept this definition of the poem. I do not see Yeats's evocation of the ladies and unicorns as a triumphant achievement of Unity of Being, but I cannot see, with Whitaker, that Yeats discredits them. The poet's title suggests the movement of the poem from hatred to a recollection of 'Heart's Fullness' and back to emptiness and sterility again. I see Yeats's vision of beauty as recollection in the midst of disorder, held precariously in the shifting cloudscape. It is interesting to note Yeats use again the pictorial and elaborate imagery of his earlier poems. The reiterated adjective 'cloud-pale' recalls the earlier 'pearl-pale hand' of 'He Gives his Beloved Certain Rhymes' (*CP*, p. 71), but here Yeats uses 'cloud-pale' to describe both a passing myth of loveliness and the disintegration of order. The 'cloud-pale rags' of the second stanza and the 'cloud-pale unicorns' of the fourth are both passing images in the poet's eye. The moon that seems 'unlike itself' moves inevitably on its cycle. It is as if Yeats is playing with images suggested by a cloud-torn sky. The procession of magical unicorns has a haunting and redeeming quality set in the midst of chaos. It is haunting because it has passed, is only half-captured and destroyed by other images as the poet moves on to tear his vision to pieces.

The fourth stanza, beginning in slow, measured contemplation of beauty, moves on with increasing plangency to the harsh blotting-out of the moon's light:

The cloud-pale unicorns, the eyes of aquamarine.
The quivering half-closed eyelids, the rags of cloud or of lace,
Or eyes that rage has brightened, arms it has made lean,
Give place to an indifferent multitude, gives place

To brazen hawks. Nor self-delighting reverie,
Nor hate of what's to come, nor pity for what's gone,
Nothing but grip of claw, and the eye's complacency,
The innumerable clanging wings that have put out the
    moon.

Yeats has presented us with the two sides of tragedy, the Vision
of Evil and Unity of Being, and he has set these in terms of the
collapse of a civilisation. Evil dominates. The closing stanza of
the poem returns us to the mind's eye. The poem offers no
solution. Its ending centres on isolation:

I turn away and shut the door, and on the stair
Wonder how many times I could have proved my
    worth
In something that all others understand or share . . . .

But he accepts struggle:

But O! ambitious heart, had such a proof drawn forth
A company of friends, a conscience set at ease,
It had but made us pine the more. The abstract joy,
The half-read wisdom of daemonic images,
Suffice the ageing man as once the growing boy.

All the poems I have discussed in this chapter, which reflects
the major preoccupations of *A Vision*, are concerned with vision,
a double vision which discovers a tension between self-expression
on the one hand and disintegration on the other. They reveal the
tragic situation as the momentary achievement of style, grace and
harmony against a background of inevitable chaos. Yeats's cyclical system necessitates a fall, a defeat, a reversal. The universe
which Yeats depicts in *A Vision* is entirely amenable to tragedy.
It makes tragedy inevitable. To sum up, we find that reality is
perceived as chaos: 'Life is no series of emanations from divine
reason . . . but an irrational bitterness, no ordinary descent from
level to level, no waterfall but a whirlpool, a gyre' (*V*, p. 40).
This vision of life as a 'whirling and a bitterness' (p. 52 and pp.
194–5) is seen as the expression of a ceaseless conflict between
opposites: desire and exhaustion of desire, the freedom of the
individual soul and 'the soul's disappearance in God' (p. 52),
unity and uniformity, birth and death, concord and discord,

phase one and phase fifteen. In Yeats's system these conflicting forces are not seen as good or evil, nor is one state the preparation for a higher. They are, rather, the two poles of the axis on which existence or the continuing cycle rotates. Yeats does suggest a contrary vision of 'ultimate reality' (p. 193) as a sphere rather than a gyre:

> The time of the development of the universe is perfect, for it is a part of nothing, it is a whole and for that reason resembles eternity. It is before all else an integrity, but only eternity confers upon existence that complete integrity which remains in itself; that of time develops, development is indeed a temporal image of that which remains complete in itself.
>
> (p. 249)

But Yeats constantly reflects that for man all things are experienced as antinomy, division and conflict. Wholeness may be glimpsed in the moment of tragedy, which is really a moment of true vision, but man is compelled to return to cycle, to defeat, to failure, to time. This characteristic double vision in which Yeats sees both wholeness, Unity of Being, integrity or delight and their opposite terrifying forces is equivalent to his later idea that we can 'embody truth' but cannot know it.[93] Truth, or the ultimate joyful reality of existence, is the whole which our divided natures and the cycles of history express through the tragic process.

4 Four Plays and the Problem of Evil

In this chapter I explore four plays: *Calvary*, *The Resurrection*, *The Words upon the Window-Pane* and *Purgatory*. These plays help to define Yeats's Vision of Evil and its place in his tragic vision. The term 'Vision of Evil' implies vision, the apocalypse which I attempted to define in the last chapter, a revelation of what *is* 'really and unchangeably' (*E&I*, p. 116). The question of evil manifests itself in two forms in Yeats's writings. First, Yeats's cyclical system, his rejection of the absolute of Christianity, is pessimistic. The ideal society has no place on earth, in heaven or in history. At moments, at the climax of a civilisation, a momentary harmony may be achieved, but its very achievement contains within it a downward pull. Chaos and anarchy must return. Within this framework the individual is forced to confront his own destruction, his own death. The Vision of Evil is at its simplest the revelation of this inevitability, darkness, frustration and defeat.

.The four plays which I discuss in this chapter fall into two pairs. The first two are concerned with panoramic vision of the cyclical movement of time, the second two with vision as what Whitaker describes as 'dramatic experience'.[1] *Calvary* and *The Resurrection* relate to Yeats's response to Christianity, to his vision of history as repeating cycle, to the theories of *A Vision*. The second pair of plays relate to Ireland, to a civilisation in decay and to the threatened turn of the cycle. But primarily they relate to the individual plight within the cycles of history and to the problem of remorse and responsibility. The first two plays affect our definition of evil. The second two compel us to experience what Yeats means by the term. In the second two, although the structure of the dance plays is abandoned, we return to the emotional landscape explored in Chapter 2. Encounters with the dark, with the Muse, with the sexual act hinted at in the

meetings of Cuchulain with the Sidhe, are central to both plays.
The encounters in these plays are placed within the context of
history repeating itself, a civilisation decaying and falling apart.
Both plays show a revulsion from life, humanity and 'the crime
of death and birth' (*CP*, p. 310). They are concerned with
frustration, remorse and desolation seen in terms of the sexual
act. Elsewhere in Yeats a very different response emerges. We
need to contrast Swift's revulsion from sexual love with a poem
such as 'Consolation' or 'The Three Bushes' or with songs from
Oedipus at Colonus. In *A Vision* (p. 52) sexual love appears as
symbol of the resolved antinomy, Unity of Being and joy. At the
same time *A Vision* balances the figures of Oedipus and Christ
and redefines their capacity for love and pity. Overshadowing all
four plays in this chapter we find the figure of Oedipus in two
roles: as the antithetical balance to the primary Christ, and as
the archetypal hero, the raging cursed scapegoat figure who yet
has the power to bless and who dies 'without the pang of death'
(*CPl*, p. 573). Oedipus is close both to Swift and to the Old Man
of *Purgatory*. Their rage is a partial and disfigured expression of
Oedipus's: 'this rage was noble, not from some general idea,
some sense of public law upheld, but because it seemed to
contain all life. . . . He knew nothing but his mind, and yet
because he spoke that mind fate possessed it' (*V*, p. 28).

Yeats's plays embody one side of the tragic predicament –
terror, evil and waste. They are, however, paths through the
tragic experience and they lead to the curious light-headed world
of *Last Poems*. At the root of Yeats's tragic antithesis between
terror and delight lies energy, full expression. The dark must be
encountered although the end may be a 'Pure, aimless joy' (*E*,
p. 489). But in exploring this Vision of Evil we must bear in
mind that Yeats sees darkness as inevitable, as a part of human
nature, a part of the nature of history. In his sense of an
inevitable cycle, in his celebration of life as drama and unending
conflict and in his sense of the hero's role expressing most fully
his personality, Yeats defies conventional concepts of good and
evil. This is reflected in critical response to Yeats's Vision of
Evil.

There are, I believe, two related problems in defining the
Vision of Evil. The first is voiced by Whitaker, who goes some
way to resolving the problem. He sees that Yeats tries to 'reconcile Christ and Lucifer', good and evil, 'the self-giving and the

self-asserting'.[2] Whitaker refers us to Buber's reaction to a similar attempt in Jung. Buber's argument is impressive:

> The soul which is integrated in the Self as the unification in all-encompassing wholeness of the opposites, especially of the opposites good and evil, dispenses with the conscience as the court which distinguishes and decides between the right and the wrong.[3]

To put this in Yeats's terms, such a man would no longer be fighting the sea. Whitaker argues that Yeats overcomes this problem by a technique of dialectical confrontation. Yeats's dialogue with history is always seen as a dialogue between two forces. In *A Vision* the dialogue is between Christ and Oedipus (not Satan or Lucifer). Whitaker argues that there is in Yeats an unsleeping conscience. Yeats glimpses, both in the pattern of history as cycle and within the individual's experience, 'the Dionysian abyss'.[4] Yeats plays with fire but thus his understanding of evil is deepened. His poems 'render and judge an evil that can be fully known only by one who has conversed with an interior Lucifer'.[5] In other words, he must go down to hell in order to reveal its horror.

The second problem is voiced by Helen Vendler. When she turns to Yeats's Vision of Evil, she does so only to dismiss it. Unlike Whitaker she does not sense any internal Lucifer. Writing of phase seventeen in *A Vision* she remarks,

> Curiously, Yeats chooses at this point to bring in a phrase we do not associate characteristically with him: 'the Vision of Evil'. . . . Certainly, if we accept his definition of the Vision of Evil – to 'conceive of the world as a continual conflict' – it is present in his own verse; but this is hardly what is usually conveyed by the phrase. Of human bonds to the earth as well as to the heavens Yeats was well aware, but the Infernos of both Dante and Blake formed no part of his cosmology.[6]

In explicating Yeats's definition of the term she suggests that Yeats substitutes an image of fruition for an image of loss. The imagination is compensatory in its actions 'so that the creative moment of greatest joy coincides with the moment of deprivation'.[7] This is to see it more or less in the same terms with which

Yeats dismisses Keats in 'Anima Hominis', and reminds us too that the Vision of Evil is hardly an uncharacteristic term for Yeats.[8] Vendler's study of 'The Soul in Judgement',[9] from which she derives Yeats's definition of evil as conflict, struggles with Yeats's treatment of remorse and expiation. She sees this bizarre purgatory as equivalent to the working of the poet's imagination as he distills images, purging them from the world of disparate experience. Though arguing that conflict is not the usual interpretation put on evil,[10] she offers no alternative definition as to what it is. All we know is that her expectations on the nature of evil are not satisfied. From evil in the life of the individual we turn to evil within the context of a cyclical system. Vendler tells us that the deluge Yeats presents in 'The Second Coming' or *The Resurrection* does not fulfil 'the characteristic function of mythical cataclysms',[11] which is to purge corruption. The cataclysm most clearly in her mind is the Judaic one. Yeats, she suggests, posits not innocence followed by evil, but two innocences. Yeats's cycles are not destroyed by wrath, not by an avenging god, but by 'necessity', 'The ceremony of innocence is drowned by a tide of anarchy which, though evil and murderous in itself, is nevertheless historically innocent, acting as an agent of inevitable historical necessity.'[12]

A. C. Bradley's criticism of Hegel throws fresh light on the problem of evil in relation to tragedy. He seems to encounter a disappointment of expectation on the nature of evil similar to that of Helen Vendler. Bradley draws attention to Hegel's definition of tragedy as conflict: 'The essentially tragic fact is the self-division and intestinal warfare of the ethical substance, not so much the war of good with evil as the war of good with good.'[13] Ideals whose nature is 'divine . . . as seen in the world of tragic action have left the repose of Olympus, have entered into human wills, and now meet as foes'.[14] Bradley concludes, however, with this: 'The last omission I would notice in Hegel's theory is that he underrates the action in tragedy of what may be called by a rough distinction moral evil rather than defect.'[15] He continues, 'If Aristotle did not in some lost part of the *Poetics* discuss ideas like this, he failed to give a complete rationale of Greek tragedy.'[16] Yet the fact is that the examples most favoured by Hegel are those of the Greek dramatists, particularly Sophocles's *Antigone*, whereas the examples Bradley gives to underline Hegel's omissions are from plays by Shakespeare, namely *Macbeth* and

Lear. It seems to me that our conceptions of what evil should be are sometimes closely related to our consciousness of the demands of Christianity and that we find difficulty in accepting a world ruled by fate rather than providence. For the Greek and the non-Christian world, the best definition of evil may well be found in the fact of conflict. It is certainly an important factor in tragedy that we see good war with good – that, for example, Richard II and Henry IV represent rival orders, both justifiable.

In *The Harvest of Tragedy* T. R. Henn presents four alternatives open to tragic vision in relation to evil.[17] First is determinism, but here there is no choice and no responsibility, hence no tragic conflict. The second hypothesis is that sin and suffering are ultimately illusory. They can be transcended. In this view, Henn argues, conflict is evaded. Only the latter two approaches really allow for tragedy. The third approach is close to Shakespearean tragedy. Henn calls this dualism:

> There is war in Heaven. God's omnipotence is only partial, or He may have withdrawn part of His omnipotence so as to clear the battleground for man. The fortunes of the battle may then ebb and flow according to man's *virtus*, his fortitude and integrity of soul. His stature as a tragic hero depends . . . upon the qualities which he exhibits in the course of his conflict.[18]

With this dualism there is the possibility of 'a free evil abroad'.[19] Like a thundercloud, any change in the pattern can set off the storm. This dualism allows for Satan and the villain. However, such a definition of evil in tragedy is still based on a conventional reading of good and evil. The fourth approach is closest to that of Yeats. Here is 'the hypothesis that the world is purposeless and chaotic'.[20] Evil is the product of change and therefore arbitrary. This is pessimism. Henn quotes,

> The sense that every struggle brings defeat
> Because Fate holds no prize to crown success
> That all the oracles are dumb or cheat
> Because they have no secret to express
> That none can pierce the vast black veils uncertain
> Because there is no light beyond the curtain
> That all is vanity and nothingness.[21]

Conflict arises because we have also to admit the sense of a creative world, 'reality and joy'.[22] This approach is close to Yeats, but, I feel, not close enough.

If we look at what the Christian world has to offer Yeats, we may come closer to an understanding of Yeats's tragic vision. Paul Tillich in *The Shaking of the Foundations* makes a clear distinction between two orders, the human–historical and the divine:

> The human order, the order of history, is primarily the order of growing and dying. 'Surely the people is grass.' Man's experience of melancholy, awakened by fading and perishing nature, is symbolic of his transitoriness. . . . There is . . . the tragic law which controls the historical process, the law which ordains that human greatness utterly fall. There is human greatness in history. . . . There are princes and even good princes; there are judges and even just judges. . . . There are creative spirits and even some which have the power of knowledge and understanding. But just in being great and powerful and righteous they touch the divine sphere, and they become arrogant, and they are brought to nothing. They are without roots; they wither; the divine storm blows over them, and they vanish. . . . They are all subject to the law of tragic self-destruction – the bad and the good, individuals and nations, the weak and the heroic.[23]

I think that this is a definition of the order of history which Yeats would have accepted with one reservation. He would agree that there is a divine order beyond the tragic human order, that

> Man transcends everything in the historical order, all the heights and depths of his own existence. He passes . . . beyond the limits of his given world. He participates in something infinite, in an order which is not transitory, not self-destructive, not tragic, but eternal, holy and blessed.[24]

Specifically Yeats would agree with Tillich that 'eternity breaks into time',[25] that a moment may contain eternity. This divine order constitutes for Yeats the momentary ecstasy of tragic joy, the delight, for example, at the close of 'Among School Children'. Turning to ethical values, Yeats would be largely in agreement with Tillich in defining the order of history as 'an order of sin and punishment',[26] an order which Tillich relates to responsibility and guilt:

> whenever I have met exiles of high moral standards and insight, I have discovered that they feel responsible for what has happened within their own countries. And very often I have met citizens of democratic countries, who have expressed a feeling of guilt for the situation of the world today. They were right . . . they are responsible. . . . Whether or not we call it sin, ... we are beaten by the consequences of our own failures. That is the order of history.[27]

This is close to Yeats's remorse and responsibility as it appears in a poem such as 'Nineteen Hundred and Nineteen' or in 'A Dialogue of Self and Soul' or 'The Man and the Echo' where:

> I lie awake night after night
> And never get the answers right. . . .
> Could my spoken words have checked
> That whereby a house lay wrecked?
> And all seems evil until I
> Sleepless would lie down and die.
> (*CP*, p. 393)

It is here that we find Whitaker's 'internal Lucifer', and, in the failure of the historical order and the remorse of the individual life, we find Yeats's Vision of Evil.

Where Yeats clearly disagrees with Tillich is in the fundamental Christian belief that God has entered history once and for all. Yeats does not disagree that Christ has entered history, but he believes in a 'Christ posed against a background not of Judaism but of Druidism, not shut off in dead history, but flowing, concrete, phenomenal' (*E&I*, p. 518). For Yeats Christ is but one expression of a diverse fountain of divinity lying at the heart of time.

Calvary was written in 1920, *The Resurrection* in 1931, but both are concerned with Yeats's response to orthodox Christianity. Both plays are concerned with the objective cycle, antipathetic to Yeats's nature, and in this antipathy lies much of his reason for rejecting Christian ethics. For Yeats, Christianity is a system of faith which denies the individual freedom and responsibility. Virtues such as good works, love and pity are scrutinised. Helen Vendler sums up Yeats's response to Christianity:

> [he] does not deny imaginative power to the primary [cycle] . . . . Yeats is not erecting a counter-system to Christianity . . . but rather abolishing imaginative monotheism in favour of a plurality of worship, since it is the single-minded devotion demanded by Christianity which is natively repugnant to Yeats's imagination.[28]

Vendler points out that both plays are set at the full moon, at phase fifteen of Yeats's cycle, despite their objective nature. Vendler sees Yeats as presenting poetic process, in this case the confrontation of two poetic traditions. In *Calvary* 'single-minded devotion' is seen as an objective demand and Yeats is intent on expressing alternative viewpoints. My point here, however, is to establish that, in rejecting Christianity's monotheism, Yeats is indeed erecting a counter-system. He is erecting a system without ultimate redemption. In Christianity Christ enters time. Yeats, however, is concerned with an eternally repeating cycle. Thus Christ's coming is one of many and the salvation he offers is limited and not all-embracing. The Christ he presents is, in fact, forsaken in a way that parodies the traditional story of the Crucifixion.

Oscar Wilde's story 'The Doer of Good' is the prime source for *Calvary*:

> Christ came from a white plain to a purple city, and as He passed through the first street He heard voices overhead, and saw a young man lying drunk upon a windowsill. 'Why do you waste your soul in drunkenness?' He said. 'Lord, I was a leper and You healed me, what else can I do?' A little further through the town He saw a young man following a harlot, and said, 'Why do you dissolve your soul in debauchery?' and the young man answered, 'Lord, I was blind, and You healed me, what else can I do?' At last in the middle of the city He saw an old man crouching, weeping upon the ground, and when He asked why he wept, the old man answered, 'Lord I was dead, and You raised me into life, what else can I do but weep?' (*A*, p. 286)[29]

Whitaker, in his study of Yeats, draws attention to another source for this play, Yeats's 'Tables of the Law', in which Aherne parallels the later role of Lazarus.[30] Aherne rejects a conventional relationship with God. He dedicates himself to the unlimited and anarchic, for 'the beautiful arts were sent into the world to overthrow nations, and finally life herself, by sowing everywhere unlimited desires, like torches thrown into a burning city' (*M*, p. 294). Yeats's quarrel with Christianity is first a quarrel with its limits. Aherne distinguishes two responses to God:

> He considered that those whose work was to live and not to reveal were children and that the Pope was their father; but he taught in secret that certain others . . . were elected, not to live, but to reveal that hidden substance of God which is colour and music and softness and a sweet odour; and that these have no father but the Holy Spirit. (p. 300)

Aherne's response is ecstatic. The children of the Holy Spirit can see the eternal and divine, 'the shining substance on which Time has heaped the refuse of creation; for the world exists to be a tale in the ears of coming generations' (ibid.). Terror, happiness, birth and death are illusory in this context. But Aherne is not able to withstand terror. He lacks Yeats's Vision of Evil. Meeting him years later we find:

> At first I was full of happiness . . . for I felt a divine ecstasy, an immortal fire in every passion, in every hope, in every desire . . . and I saw, in the shadows under the leaves, in the hollow waters, in the eyes of men and women, its image, as in a mirror . . . . (p. 304)

Whitaker comments,

> The gnostic God sees in the glittering satanic folds of the temporal world a dark yet beautiful reflection of his own image. So it was with Aherne in the first flush of ecstasy. But, because a finite ego cannot endure isolation in a mirroring labyrinth . . . it has what Yeats would call in *The King's Threshold*, 'The hunger of the crane, that starves himself / At

the full moon because he is afraid / Of his own shadow in the glittering water . . . .'[31]

Aherne in 'The Tables of the Law' finds his first ecstasy change to misery. He has made himself immortal in desire and yet remains mortal. He can no longer sin because he is his own expression, self-complete, but 'God has made a simple and an arbitrary law that we may sin and repent' (*M*, p. 305). Aherne learns that there is a distinction between angels, who need only to hope for, desire and dream of the immortal, and men, who are tied to their mortality as to their bodies. Aherne has exiled himself from the one world but does not belong in the other: 'I am not among those for whom Christ died' (ibid.). There are in fact two ways of comprehending God, as Holy Ghost or as the Father. Aherne can relinquish neither. Aherne recalls Yeats's description of his friends in 'The Tragic Generation', particularly the Johnson of 'Dark Angel' with its tortured and perverted relationship with Christianity:

> Nor will thine envious heart allow
> Delight untortured by desire.
> Through thee, the gracious Muses turn
> To Furies, O mine Enemy!
> And all the things of beauty burn
> With flames of evil ecstacy.
> (Lionel Johnson's 'Dark Angel',
> quoted in *A*, p. 314)

And Yeats asks, 'Why are these strange souls born everywhere today, with hearts that Christianity, as shaped by history, cannot satisfy?' (p. 315).

In *Calvary* (*CPl*, pp. 449–57) Yeats counterpoints two imaginative possibilities and this lends as much pathos to Christ as to Lazarus or to the heron: 'God has not died for the white heron.' The tragedy here is, as in Wilde's story, not only that of Lazarus, but also that of Christ, for in both the story and the play Christ is confronted with his own failure. The opening song presents us with an image of isolation and fixation:

> Motionless under the moonbeam
> Up to his feathers in the stream

> Although fish leap, the white heron
> Shivers in a dumb-founded dream.

The heron is trapped within the objective cycle. Yeats's notes on the play tell us that

> Certain birds, especially as I see things, such lonely birds as the heron, hawk, eagle and swan, are the natural symbols of subjectivity . . . while the beasts that run upon the ground, especially those that run in packs, are the natural symbols of objective man.   (*VPl*, p. 789)

Yeats suggests a further release with the turn of the cycle: 'But that the full is shortly gone'. The heron is ultimately presented as free, particularly in the closing song, which, though melancholy, is a song of flight. The heron is related to images of the swan and to the hawk in 'On a Political Prisoner' (*CP*, p. 206). Yeats's notes tell us that the birds in his song are used to 'increase the objective loneliness of Christ by contrasting it with a loneliness . . . that unlike His can be, whether joyous or sorrowful, sufficient to itself':

> I have surrounded Him with the images of those He cannot save, not only with the birds . . . but with Lazarus and Judas and the Roman soldiers for whom He has died in vain. 'Christ', writes Robartes, 'only pitied those whose suffering is rooted in death, in poverty, or in sickness, or in sin, in some shape of the common lot, and he came especially to the poor who are most subject to exterior vicissitude'. I have therefore represented in Lazarus and Judas types of that intellectual despair that lay beyond His sympathy, while in the Roman soldiers I suggest a form of objectivity that lay beyond His help.   (*VPl*, p. 790)

Christ becomes an anti-hero in this play. Yeats, moreover, undermines accepted definitions of moral virtues, definitions of pity and love. In *A Vision*, for example, Yeats describes Christ thus:

> We say of Him because His sacrifice was voluntary that He was Love itself, and yet that part of Him that made Christendom

was not love but pity, and not pity for intellectual despair . . .
but *primary* pity, that for the common lot, man's death, seeing
that He raised Lazarus, sickness, seeing that He healed many,
sin, seeing that He died.   (p. 275)

Yeats draws a distinction between love, which he sees as subjective, and pity of this primary kind:

Love is created and preserved by intellectual analysis, for we
love only that which is unique, and it belongs to contemplation, not to action, for we would not change that which we
love. A lover will admit a greater beauty than that of his
mistress but not its like . . . .   (Ibid.)

Antithetical pity is directed away from the common: 'he pities
only if something threatens that which has never been before and
can never be again' (ibid.).
    In the play Christ is confronted with mockery. First we hear
the conventional story, the crowd shouting 'Work a miracle'. But
Lazarus, who is evidence of such a miracle, deepens the mockery
of the crowd:

Alive I never could escape your love,
And when I sickened towards my death I thought,
'I'll to the desert, or chuckle in a corner,
Mere ghost, a solitary thing.' . . .
You dragged me to the light as boys drag out
A rabbit when they have dug its hole away.

Lazarus hopes to find in Christ's death a return to his own
solitude, an escape from Christ's all-embracing and objective
pity. Christ cannot even understand Lazarus's demands for
privacy. Although Christ tells him, 'I have conquered death, /
And all the dead shall be raised up again', he has failed, for
Lazarus rejects the very idea of salvation:

Make way for Lazarus that must go search
Among the desert places where there is nothing
But howling wind and solitary birds.

With Lazarus's departure Yeats returns to the traditional story.
Martha and Mary come to grieve at the impending death of

Christ. They are not visually present and are created in the mind's eye by the musician:

> Their lips are pressed and their tears fall; and now
> They cast them on the ground before His dirty
> Blood-dabbled feet and clean them with their hair.

They alone are dependent on Christ's love. Without it they are spent, cast out into the heron's world of solitude in which they have no part:

> Take but His love away,
> Their love becomes a feather . . . .

But with their departure comes a sense of final doom,

> I felt their hair upon my feet a moment
> And then they fled away – why have they fled?

Judas enters. He represents intellectual despair for Yeats, but he is the least convincing figure in the play. In the traditional story Judas, with his anger at money wasted that should have been spent on the poor, would appear to belong far more to the objective world than Christ does. Yet Yeats presents Lazarus and Judas as twin figures of despair, the one condemned to live, the other taking his own life. Judas deprives Christ of his absolute power. He finds an escape: 'Whatever man betrays Him will be free'. Finally he mocks Christ: 'and now / You cannot even save me'.

Yeats presents the Roman soldiers in their traditional role. They gamble for Christ's clothes and are utterly indifferent to him. Yeats's notes tell us that they represent an objectivity beyond Christ's power. Their indifference stands, I think, for the relentless turning of the gyre, its mechanistic inevitability:

> They say you're good and that you made the world,
> But it's no matter. . . .

> One thing is plain,
> To know that he has nothing that we need
> Must be a comfort to him.

Yeats's dance again operates as an irony. Here it is not un-
fulfilled desire as in the earlier dance plays, but indifference,
idiotic rigmarole:

> In the dance
> We quarrel for a while, but settle it
> By throwing dice, and after that, being friends,
> Join hand to hand and wheel about the cross.

Their dance is predestined, but not in Christ's terms. Yeats
finally twists the traditional story: 'My father, why hast Thou
forsaken Me?' Christ's loneliness upon the cross seems almost to
transform him to his antithesis, the solitary heron.

In the closing song the subjective world is set free. The whole
action of the play leads up to this. The objective moon becomes
its opposite subjective self:

FIRST MUSICIAN.
> The ger-eagle has chosen his part
> In blue deep of the upper air
> Where one-eyed day can meet his stare;
> He is content with his savage heart.

SECOND MUSICIAN.
> God has not appeared to the birds.

THIRD MUSICIAN.
> But where have last year's cygnets gone?
> The lake is empty; why do they fling
> White wing out beside white wing?
> What can a swan need but a swan?

The human world is deserted. Yeats returns to the solitary figure
of the swan and the idea of the world as its reflection, a world
which veers between the 'savage heart' content with itself and
the heron who 'Shivers in a dumb-founded dream'. This desolate
world, whether defiant or half-crazed, is utterly opposed to the
Christian order of sin and salvation.

Compared with the earlier dance plays, *Calvary* is unsatisfying
despite its momentary pathos at the ironic transfiguration of
Christ and despite the way in which Yeats weaves the thread of

the traditional story only to lure us to antithesis, to bring us with a shock to another point of view. Yeats does not really succeed in appropriating Christ as he can such a figure as Swift. The emotional and spiritual power of Calvary itself overshadows the poet and his play does not provide us with an alternative imaginative world. The play is really a framework for Yeats's theories about Christianity, his dissatisfactions with its demands of 'single-minded devotion'.

With *The Resurrection* Yeats turns again to Christ. But in this play Yeats explores the myth of creation. Each cycle in Yeats's system springs from a tumultuous reversal and overturning in which the world is created anew. Each new cycle is heralded by an annunciation of a new divinity. Each divinity is unique and yet repeats a past pattern; the pattern of God's death and rebirth is ritual for ever being re-enacted. In this context some definition of myth will be helpful. In *The Catholic Encyclopaedia* a distinction is drawn between historical truth and mythical truth:

> Myth of its very nature repels historicity, because the event it relates happened before history began, in an eternal instant . . . . Myth does not explain so much as it reveals and is unconcerned about apparent contradictions, because such contradictions exist in the empirical realm only.[32]

History can be seen as a linear progression of time and it is in this sense that Yeats rejects conventional readings of history. It is here too that he quarrels with Christianity. In it Christ and God are rooted in time. In *The Resurrection* Yeats focuses on the heart of time, the moment of revelation, the first phase. The main concern of the play is with man's response to this moment, which is an upheaval of all established ways of comprehending the world. An apparent linear progression reaching its climax in the 'civilised' world of the Roman Empire is shattered, brought to nothing. Chaos returns.

Yeats's notes on the play tell us of his struggle for belief and his rejection of the myth of progress. He traces the growth within himself of a counter-myth. That is the myth of reversal accompanied by a 'laughing, ecstatic destruction' (*VPl*, p. 932). Yeats's response to this reversal is ambiguous. The play presents the risen Christ as a new incarnation, a reversal of the classical wheel, and, though this heralds an 'objective' era distasteful to the poet, it is welcomed as an example of cyclical reversal. Although rooted in history, this reversal is a partial expression of a central unchanging truth. By seeing the stasis of the temporal world the poet comes to a kind of freedom. He is no longer trapped in a blind belief in historical progress. Yeats argues,

> Even though we think temporal existence illusionary it cannot be capricious; it is what Plotinus called the characteristic act of the soul and must reflect the soul's coherence. . . . We may come to think that nothing exists but a stream of souls, that all knowledge is biography. . . . Such belief may arise from Communism by antithesis, declaring at last even to the common ear, that all things have a value according to the clarity of their expression of themselves, and not as functions of changing economic conditions or as a preparation for some Utopia. There is perhaps no final happy state except in so far as men may grow gradually better; escape may be for individuals alone who know how to exhaust their possible lives, to set, as it were, the hands of the clock racing.   (pp. 934–5)

The first part of this argument is clarified in a passage from *A Vision*, where Yeats talks of the concept of development as 'a temporal image' of the eternal, of wholeness and integrity (p. 249). The closest man may come to such an integrity is the closest he can come to a full expression of himself, the full exhaustion of all possibilities open to him. Development is not linear progress, but complete self-expression and 'There is . . . no final happy state.' Yeats's morality turns aside from good works in favour of completion. Yeats rejects the treatment of man as function, even of a good cause: 'Even our best histories treat men as function. Why must I think the victorious cause the better? . . . I am satisfied . . . to find but drama . . . . No battle has been finally won or lost . . .' (*VPl*, p. 935). Yeats substitutes drama and unending conflict for the preparation of any utopia. *The Resurrection* presents a drama of change and defeat. The Greek world falls, just as in *Calvary* Christ's world fails as an absolute.

Helen Vendler dismisses Yeats's treatment of history in *A Vision*: 'Any essay that attempts to scan the years from 2000 B. C. to A. D. 2000 in thirty pages must be sketchy, to say the least.'[33] The importance of Yeats's use of history, she argues, is 'to convey his sense of the power and order of the creative act'.[34] At the centre of this act lies 'the Heraclitean reciprocal relationship in which two nations "die each other's life, live each other's death"':[35]

> Yeats's schemes, then, far from being a tiresome, successive record of birth, maturity, and death, affirm the simultaneity of these events . . . Yeats gets most of his best poetic effects from his reciprocal symbols of birth and death. Always he insists that one is symbolic of the other, that the two are not only concomitant but identical.[36]

Such a reciprocal relationship lies at the centre of *The Resurrection*, and I do not think it is necessary to limit its range of implications to any narrow reading of the 'creative act', for the play is a re-creation of the resurrected God.

Whitaker sees Yeats's use of history operate in two ways: as 'dramatic experience' and as 'panoramic vision'. Panoramic vision of the whole frees us from the illusion of time. Whitaker allies this to contemplation, which

> though not wilful is not passive or static. In fact, if we renounce the desire to remake the world, we may learn how to change it in the only possible way. For when ego abdicates, it frees a deeper self which is 'not I' – a self which can say 'we would not change that which we love', and which therefore can allow the forces of a continual creation to flow through it. Most artists seem to have recognised this as a paradoxical fact of experience.[37]

Whitaker sees these two ways of exploring history as typical of Yeats. In the opening song of *The Resurrection* (*CPL*, pp. 579–94) we move, as in 'Leda and the Swan' from emphatic identification to a more detached or Olympian view.

The opening song transforms the gentle wonder we met in 'The Mother of God':

> What is this flesh I purchased with my pains,
> This fallen star my milk sustains,
> This love that makes my heart's blood stop
> Or strikes a sudden chill into my bones
> And bids my hair stand up?
>
> > (*CP*, p. 282)

Christ's birth is presented as savage. A vision is directly presented with an emphatic 'I saw'. This is unlike the musicians' songs in other plays, which suggest doubt and hesitation. Another difference lies in the setting. In earlier plays the musicians called to mind a specific place, creating this in the mind's eye. Here the song dazzles us with the light of heaven, with a panoramic vista of history. We are not in any specific place, but men on earth under the heavens:

> I saw a staring virgin stand
> Where holy Dionysius died,
> And tear the heart out of his side,
> And lay the heart upon her hand
> And bear that beating heart away;
> And then did all the Muses sing
> Of Magnus Annus at the spring,
> As though God's death were but a play.

The staring form, the beating heart, holy Dionysius – all put Mary into the context of savage ritual. Enacting this ritual we are at the beginning, at the birth of every cycle. Anthony Bradley argues that Yeats here attempts to show us that Christ's death and resurrection

> are not unique . . . but typical of all the gods of these mystery religions. As with Dionysius, Attis, Adonis, and Osiris, Christ's death and resurrection is a spiritual equivalent to the fertility myth that describes the great cycle of palingenesis, that is, the death of the natural world in winter and its resurrection in spring.[38]

The major difference between Christianity and such primitive religions lies in Christian ethics. Bradley suggests that by Victorian times Christ's Godhead had come to take second place beside the usefulness of the moral doctrine. Yeats is rebelling against this. Bradley suggests that the relative barbarism of the opening song and the intrusion of drums from the Dionysian mobs during the action of the play should suggest: 'to an alert audience that Christianity may retain some of the barbarism so obviously excluded from it by the humanist and rational conceptions of the play's two main characters'.[39]

In the second stanza of the opening song the tone of participation is replaced by a more panoramic and distant view, which takes within its scope the fall of the Greek civilisation and which prophesies the fall of the new:

> Another Troy must rise and set,
> Another lineage feed the crow,
> Another Argo's painted prow
> Drive to a flashier bauble yet.

Then Yeats presents the particular moment in time, the Roman epoch in shock at change and the ensuing collapse of its order:

> The Roman Empire stood appalled:
> It dropped the reins of peace and war
> When that fierce virgin and her Star
> Out of the fabulous darkness called.

The play that follows seems a little thin in comparison. Yet we must move through the play to understand the progression in the closing song. The three protagonists are named only by type – Hebrew, Greek and Syrian. They are the last remnants of the crowd which has followed Christ and they are guarding the disciples. The atmosphere is confused. All is sudden noise and rumour. Dionysius's followers are wandering through the streets like a pack of wolves. There is a rumour that 'the dead had broken out of the cemeteries'. Against this turbulent background, the Hebrew and Greek strive, in their different ways, to retain a vision which no longer reflects their changing world. The Hebrew depicts himself as a practical man. In contrast to the apostles, he sees himself as responsible, rejecting extremes: 'for the Eleven it was always complete light or complete darkness'. He has seen a dead man being buried. For him it is a case of an understandable megalomania:

> He was nothing more than a man, the best man who ever
> lived. Nobody before him had so pitied human misery. . . .
> Then some day when he was very tired, after a long journey
> perhaps, he thought that he himself was the Messiah. He
> thought it because of all destinies it seemed the most terrible.

The Hebrew, here, is propagating Yeats's theory of the mask, the choosing of 'all destinies, the most terrible'. He cannot make the leap that man may become his Daimon, his anti-self. For him, as for the Greek, man and God are separate. The Greek, on the other hand, sees only the divine in Christ:

> I am laughing because they thought they were nailing the hands of a living man upon the Cross, and all the time there was nothing there but a phantom. . . . We Greeks understand these things. No god has ever been buried: no god has ever suffered. Christ only seemed to be born, ... only seemed to die.

The Hebrew outlines the objective revelation, the demands of one God. His unwillingness to recognise the divine in Christ is, as Helen Vendler points out,[40] the position of an objective mind which yet fears the unknown revelation; but it also illustrates the complete sacrifice demanded by the objective cone: 'One had to give up all worldly knowledge, all ambition, do nothing of one's own will. Only the divine could have any reality. God had to take complete possession.' The Greek totally rejects the objective cycle. Like Lazarus, he cannot abide the notion of a corporate body of sin and suffering. He argues, 'Every man's sins are his property. Nobody else has a right to them.' For him the gods are many rather than one and their relationship with man respects man's privacy:

> They can be discovered by contemplation, in their faces a high keen joy like the cry of a bat, and the man who lives heroically gives them the only earthly body that they covet. He, as it were, copies their gestures and their acts. What seems their indifference is but their eternal possession of themselves. Man too remains separate. He does not surrender his soul. He keeps his privacy.

The excesses of the Dionysian mob disgust the Greek. He recognises the custom which they are celebrating: 'Three days after the full moon, a full moon in March, they sing the death of the god and pray for his resurrection.' But he rejects them: 'I cannot think all that self-surrender and self-abasement is Greek, despite the Greek name of its god.' The Greek would remain with civilisation at its fifteenth phase. He does not want the cycle to turn. He is in fact ignorant of the cycle, and it is the later actions of the play which enlighten him.

When the Syrian enters he disproves both Greek and Hebrew, for Christ has rolled back the stone from his tomb and 'A hand without bones, without sinews, cannot move a stone.' The Syrian reflects the mob outside. He has lost control of himself. He is laughing, he appears drunk. The play reads, at this point, like a page from *A Vision* divided between voices. To the question, 'What is knowledge?', we have two answers. Knowledge is what makes up civilisation and order; knowledge is progress. It has 'made the modern world, that stands between us and the barbarian'. The second response suggests that knowledge is limited: 'What if there is always something that lies outside knowledge, outside order? What if at the moment when knowledge and order seem complete that something appears?' The laughter of the Syrian, the drums and rattles of the Dionysian frenzy all speak of a giving-way, a loss of control, and then, of a sudden, stillness falls:

> How they roll their painted eyes as the dance grows quicker and quicker! . . . Why are they all suddenly motionless? Why are all those unseeing eyes turned upon this house? Is there anything strange about this house?

The Hebrew answers, 'Somebody has come into the room.' The words of argument peter out. As in 'The Second Coming' and as in 'Leda and the Swan', Yeats presents the appearance of the divine as grotesque and horrifying. The Greek expects the phantom, like Fand and the Sidhe, to exist on a separate level:

> There is nothing here but a phantom, it has no flesh and blood. Because I know the truth I am not afraid. Look, I will touch it. It may be hard under my hand like a statue – I have heard of such things – or my hand may pass through it – but there is no flesh and blood.

His horror mirrors the horror of the Boy in *Purgatory*, 'A dead, living, murdered man' (*CPL*, p. 687). He learns of the irrational, the supernatural: 'God and man die each other's life, live each other's death.'

The closing song and the act of folding and unfolding the cloth once again distance us from the action:

In pity for man's darkening thought
He walked that room and issued thence
In Galilean turbulence;
The Babylonian starlight brought
A fabulous, formless darkness in;
Odour of blood when Christ was slain
Made all Platonic tolerance vain
And vain all Doric discipline.

In the final stanza talk of God turns to talk of man. The play has shown the human and divine as inextricably linked. In this final stanza imagination made of both is celebrated. Whitaker notes Yeats's skill in presenting us with a fall in terms that imply resurrection.[41] Beginning with man's exhaustion, the stanza moves on to celebrate,

Whatever flames upon the night
Man's own resinous heart has fed.

He comments that 'the "beating heart" of the first song and the "resinous heart" of the second are partial images for the same inexplicable force': 'To the complaint that this is a mystery, that Christ or Dionysius must be either God or Man, the play itself retorts by disposing of those rational heresies . . . held by Greek and Hebrew.'[42] One must add that the closing stanza with its sinking and closing movement reflects on the stanza before it, making clear that Christ's rebirth is part of a process in which

Everything that man esteems
Endures a moment or a day . . . .

The disappointment and renewal of man's labours throughout imagined history is central to Yeats's tragic vision. He presents a 'play'. He is satisfied with drama. His emphasis is on energy and exhaustion. Every undertaking contains the seeds of its own destruction.

Yeats's Introduction (*VPl*, pp.937–77) to *The Words upon the Window-Pane* summarises his response to history in the secular sense, where *Calvary* and *The Resurrection* summarise his response to history in the religious sense. Yeats sees a choice between 'three ideas of national life: that of Swift; that of a great Italian of his day; that of modern England' (*VPl*, p. 957). Yeats's Swift offers the reader something which tends to be obscured in *A Vision* with its stress on recurring wheels and cycle: the notion of responsibility which depends upon integrity. Swift's was the 'one Irish century that escaped from darkness and confusion' (*VPl*, p. 958). It was a century with enormous intellectual and imaginative scope. It marked

> the spread of science and of scholarship over Europe, its examination of documents, its destruction of fables, a science and a scholarship modern for the first time, of certain great minds that were medieval in their scope but modern in their freedom. (Ibid.)

Yeats recognises it as a time of a magnificent sense of confidence. He recalls 'the palace of Blenheim, its pride of domination that expected a thousand years' (p. 959). Yet the modern world that swept over Ireland with the Battle of the Boyne, overwhelming 'a civilisation full of religion and myth', was largely antipathetic to Yeats with its 'intelligible laws planned out upon a great blackboard, [its] capacity for horizontal lines . . . for attitudes of mind that could be multiplied like an expanding bookcase' (ibid.). The true heir of this might be Shaw, whom Yeats half admires and half detests and whom in *Autobiographies* he envisages as a sewing-machine 'that clicked and shone . . . and smiled perpetually' (p. 283). But there was also in the dawning of the modern world a moment of true renaissance, 'something that appeared and perished in its dawn, an instinct for Roman rhetoric, Roman elegance' (*VPl*, p. 959). This modern tide, at its start less filthy, gave Ireland a new aristocracy, a new parliament and the birth of political nationality. For Swift this was won out of 'action and passion', for Berkeley 'through contemplation'. A vigorous transformation occurred, 'a general stir of life'; building, metalwork, music and science flourished. But the moment was followed by Ireland's 'dark insipid period' and the Act of Union (p. 960). Yeats's fascination with Swift lies in Swift's sense of imminent doom: 'He foresaw the ruin to come' (ibid.). Yeats's undergraduate, Corbet, catalogues the elements of that ruin – democracy, the French Revolution: 'the common run of men, – "I hate lawyers, I hate doctors" he said, "though I love Dr. So-and-So and Judge So-and-So"' (ibid.). *Gulliver's*

Travels was the product of Swift's rage at this devastation, his *saeva indignatio* which justified 'the greatest epitaph in history' (*VPl*, pp. 960–1).

Yeats turns to Swift's 'Discourse of the Contests and Dissensions between the Nobles and the Commons in Athens and Rome'[43] to illustrate the argument against democracy. The health of a state depends upon a balance between the One, the Few and the Many. Ideally 'The One is the executive . . . ; the Few are those who through the possession of hereditary wealth, or great personal gifts, have come to identify their lives with the life of the State, whereas the lives and ambitions of the Many are private' (*VPl*, p. 961). The Many are singular 'in action and in thought' and do not copy their wisest neighbour. But if they are put 'to the work of the State' that independence vanishes. Each, 'listed in a party', 'becomes the fanatical follower of men of whose characters he knows next to nothing, and from that day on puts nothing in his mouth that some other man has not already chewed and digested' (ibid.). But in Swift's reading of civilisation the ideal balance is far from lasting. And, though good management can prolong order, it cannot uphold it for ever.[44] The typical end of a civilisation is 'Tyranny'. For Swift 'all forms of government must be mortal like their authors'; the seeds of its destruction are sown at its birth and destroy it 'as rust eats away iron, and worms devour wood' (ibid.).

The second idea or choice facing the Ireland of Yeats's day belongs to Vico, and Yeats sees it as the background to the dominance of Mussolini (p. 962). Vico's theory has much in common with Swift's in that, for both, different types of government replace one another. But Vico supports the rise of the Many: 'He thought civilisation passed through the phases Swift has described, but that it was harsh and terrible until the Many prevailed, and its joints cracked and loosened' (ibid.). The crucial difference – Swift seeing 'civilisation pass from comparative happiness and youthful vigour to an old age of violence and self-contempt', Vico seeing it 'begin in penury like himself and end as he himself would in a long inactive peace' (ibid.) – lies in their differing responses to morality. Swift ascribed the process 'to virtues and vices all could understand', but Vico saw it as 'the rhythm of the elemental forms of the mind' (ibid.). The two are not necessarily contradictory, but the second view establishes the process as automatic, hence beyond good and evil.

Yeats's response veers from the one to the other, close to Vico with his 'elemental forms', with 'the murderous innocence of the sea', with the framework of *A Vision*; but close to Swift in his delineation of personality, in his creation of a tragic hero, in his conflict with the annihilating sea, in his celebration of the aristocratic mien, in his recognition of responsibility and choice, and in his frequent, though ambiguous, horror at the anarchy which accompanies the turning of the cycle. Yeats concludes,

> Some philosopher has added this further thought: the classes rise out of the matrix, create all mental and bodily riches, sink back, as Vico saw civilisation rise and sink, and government is there to keep the ring and see to it that combat never ends. (*VPl*, p. 962)

Again the emphasis is on drama, unending conflict, energy and full expression of the personality.

The third choice is progress, which both Swift's and Vico's philosophies discredit. They after all 'have already deepened our sense of tragedy' (ibid.). Yeats urges us to accept this tragic code, this belief in 'the eternal circuit', because it best suits 'our pre-occupation with the soul's salvation, our individualism, our solitude' (p. 963). This 'we' to whom Yeats refers is the Irish race. Now the doctors and lawyers whom Swift detested, the specialised and abstract forces of society, dominate: 'man ceased to think; his work thought in him' (p. 964). Spinoza, Berkeley, Swift, Goethe 'recognised no compulsion but the "bent and current" of their lives' (ibid.). But now 'the best modern philosophers are professors', while poet and artist are 'separated spirits' (ibid.). Yeats concludes his discussion of Swift's philosophy, theory of history and the intellect by returning to Swift's mythic proportions. Just as Synge many years earlier had been linked with Shakespeare, Dante and Goethe by re-creating man 'not through the eyes or in history but . . . in the depths of the mind' (*E&I*, p. 341), so Swift in the company of Spinoza, the Masons and Berkeley 'stood there free at last from all prepossessions and touched the extremes of thought' (*VPl*, p. 965). The relative success or failure of their beliefs and schemes is irrelevant. 'Time' is 'broken away from their feet' (ibid.).

Yeats's Introduction closes with a return to Swift's personality – to his madness and to his sexual life, both of which reflect a response to life as horrifying and repugnant. In this rage at life and flesh we come close to Yeats's Vision of Evil. The play *The Words upon the Window-Pane* is concerned more closely and more overtly with this aspect of Swift than with his philosophical life. Yet the horror, Swift's refusal to beget children and his madness, is an expression of the turning of the cycle: 'Was Swift mad? Or was it the intellect itself that was mad?'

Before beginning my discussion of the play it will be helpful to examine two critical responses. Douglas N Archibald, in his discussion of the play, suggests that it involves a tension between three images of Swift:

> The public figure imagined and discussed by Corbet is at the height of his power; the man loved by Stella and Vanessa is past his prime but not yet sunk 'into imbecility or madness'; the aged, deformed, and demented apparition is the dying dean of legend and fact.[45]

Archibald isolates Swift's chief significance for Yeats as a powerful image 'of despair and suffering'. He argues that 'Yeats has a problem: how to affirm life without dismissing Swift'.[46] In summary

> Swift has broadened [Yeats's] idea of tragedy and enabled him to make it a concrete part of Anglo-Irish history and his own heritage. He had to come to grips with Swiftean despair and wanted to endorse Swiftean indignation. The encounter with Swift gave Yeats a powerful emblem with which to stiffen his own and his country's backbone; it also made more urgent his need to face 'the desolation of reality' and to transform it, to transfigure dread by gaiety.[47]

In *W. B. Yeats and the Theatre of Desolate Reality* David Clark offers a comprehensive and acute analysis of the play. He concentrates largely on technique and on the play's relation to the historical process. He compares the method of presentation with *The Dreaming of the Bones*, where, he argues, the objective world floods in:

> In *The Words upon the Window-Pane* the opposite situation is found. As the spirit of Swift interrupts a modern séance,

reliving the Stella–Vanessa story, it is the too solid world of actuality whose limits must be rent to let knowledge flow in from the world of spiritual existences. Similarly, the superficially accurate reporting of the prose is broken by lines from a poem, a hymn, an epitaph and the Bible, lines which communicate a deeper level.[48]

Clark argues that Yeats's use of prose is suited to his Augustan subject. This prose is, however, used in a very complex manner: 'Yeats achieves intensity by multiplying the contexts within which his prose must be heard. Interest is shifted from richness of language to richness of significance, from the expression to the dramatised image or idea.'[49] The chief tool to this end is Yeats's use of myth. Clark isolates five dominant myths: *A Vision* and history as cycle; a myth of the eighteenth century and Swift's expression of Irish nationality; an Augustan myth – 'As Yeats regards Swift, so Swift regards Brutus and Ancient Rome'; the Christian myth; and the older myth of spiritualism. Clark notes how Yeats makes use of proper names, town names, family names, names of teashops and heroic names.[50] In conclusion Clark sums up the achievement of this play:

The play takes Ibsen's set – the parlour with a window on the void – and uses it for Yeats's own purposes. In Ibsen there is nothing – vast cultural and spiritual blank beyond the window. In Yeats it is beyond the 'window-pane' that the real world of spiritual existences has its being. The words on the window-pane carry us to the moment of perception. . . . The convention communicates the idea of a lack of vision – quite ironic in this situation. . . . Yeats picks the occasion – a séance – where all circumstantial realism will testify against its own completeness or sufficiency as truth. Swift, the most 'real' presence in the play, never appears on the stage.[51]

But when Clark turns to confront this central figure he detects certain ironies in Yeats's treatment of Swift. First, Swift's epitaph is disproved. Swift has not achieved a rest from *saeva indignatio*. Secondly, the play disproves Swift's Augustan self, which would not have countenanced the supernatural. Clark sees Swift's purgatory in this play as enigmatic: 'What crime has Swift committed that he must suffer in this Purgatory until God

gives peace?'[52] He suggests tentatively that Swift has denied
God's chance, electing only for choice. Swift's refusal to gamble
with the ivory dice, his rejection of Vanessa and sexual life, is
perhaps his crime:

> Did he not through his hatred and fear of the irrational
> commit a crime against the teeming life of 'the sacred earth'? I
> do not mean to put a moralistic interpretation upon Swift's
> tragedy, but it may be that in rejecting sex and the future,
> Swift was rejecting the thirteenth sphere in which man's
> freedom from the deterministic cycles inheres.[53]

Swift's suffering, his remorse, is the central vision of the play. I
cannot accept Clark's tentative interpretation. Swift's tragedy *is*
his suffering, his remorse, his madness, his blood-sodden heart
that drags him down into mankind. The only moral interpretation possible is a criticism of tragedy itself. Swift's purgatory,
his tragedy *is* the future, hostile, alien, insane and inescapable.
Torchiana points out Yeats's comments on Swift in a letter
which draws our attention to the idea of the scapegoat:

> When a [man] of Swift's sort is born into . . . dryness, is he not
> in the Catholic sense of the word its *victim*? A French Catholic
> priest once told me of certain holy women. One was victim for
> a whole country, another for such and such a village. Is not
> Swift the human soul in that dryness, is not that his tragedy
> and his genius? Perhaps every historical phase may have its
> victim – its poisoned rat in a hole. (*L*, p. 819)[54]

In my reading of the play I see Swift's role as victim and
scapegoat as central. In view of Clark's comprehensive analysis
of the techniques used in the play and the play's treatment of the
historical myth, I do not intend to go over this ground again.
Instead I shall concentrate on Swift's remorse, his relationship
with Stella and Vanessa, his madness and the area of vision
beyond the window-pane. This play and *Purgatory* introduce us
to a mental landscape of suffering, a heightened state of intensity
in which each central figure utters an apocalyptic vision of
darkness and loss. I believe that Yeats's esoteric theories as we
meet them in 'The Soul in Judgement' or in his explorations of
spiritualism and séance can best be understood as an attempt to
chart such intense mental and emotional landscapes.

In addition to Yeats's remarks on mediumship in the Introduction to the play, a useful prologue can be found in the essay
'Swedenborg, Mediums and the Desolate Places', to which I
drew attention in Chapter 2. What is important here is a
redefinition of good and evil. The spirit world or the landscapes
which the spirit inhabits are self-chosen and self-created. In the
Introduction to the play Yeats again draws attention to Swedenborg's more conventional notions of good and evil. He 'denounced
all spirits that had not reached their final rest for jugglers and
cheats' (*VPl*, p. 972). Yeats's response to the question of mediumship is ambiguous. Ellmann sums up the truth when he tells us,
'Yeats more and more inclined to the use of myth and metaphor
which somersaulted over the question of literal belief.'[55] In his
Introduction Yeats comments on mediumship with a scepticism
which finally disarms itself. He argues that all mediumship is
dramatisation, and hence 'even honest mediums cheat at times
either deliberately or because some part of the body has freed
itself from the control of the waking will' (p. 968). Yeats's
concern is with the area explored when the body is set free from
the everyday. There is evidence for some mystery here: 'what
shall we say of their knowledge of events, their assumption of
forms and names beyond the mediums's knowledge or ours?'
(ibid.). This area of mystery, as Yeats's argument progresses, is
linked to the Daimonic Memory, the shared memory lying at the
heart of reality.

Yeats posits an Indian ascetic who tells of a state where
'thought and existence are the same'. This state, 'a death-like
trance' is very close to the actions of those spirits who experience
Yeats's purgatory in *A Vision*. In trance

> They examine their past if undisturbed by our importunity,
> tracing events to their source, and as they take the form their
> thought suggests, seem to live backward through time; or if
> incapable of such examination, creatures not of thought but of
> feeling, renew as shades certain detached events of their past
> lives, taking the greater excitements first. (*VPl*, p. 968)

Relating this process to 'The Soul in Judgement', we see that the
spirit must replay his life in all its intensity, becoming the victim
where he had been torturer and *vice versa*. Such a process,
whether or not we accept or dismiss a literal belief in spirits,
hauntings, séances and reincarnation, is ultimately a process of

self-exploration, a full realisation of one's nature and personality. Thus a spirit may be forced into rocky and desolate places and to experience suffering, remorse and loss. Swift, I feel, is to be judged in this way and not as being punished for a failure to gamble on life.

Yeats allies the world of trance and medium with the daimonic:

> It is fitting that Plotinus should have been the first philosopher to meet his daimon face to face . . . for he was the first to establish as sole source the timeless individuality or daimon instead of the Platonic Idea, to prefer Socrates to his thought. This timeless individuality contains archetypes of all possible existences whether of man or of brute . . . .   (pp. 969–70)

Yeats concludes with an appeal for the recognition of this 'timeless individuality' which cuts across time and circumstance and in so doing he would reveal a world far removed from that of Swift's sufferings in that it provides a whole rather than a partial vision:

> If we accept this idea many strange or beautiful things become credible. . . . All about us there seems to start up a precise, inexplicable, teeming life, and the earth becomes once more, not in rhetorical metaphor, but in reality, sacred.   (p. 970)

The opening of *The Words upon the Window-Pane* (*CPl*, pp. 597–617) introduces us to the two major themes, the strange world of the spirit or the dead and to the character of Swift. John Corbet, a Cambridge undergraduate who is writing a thesis on Swift, is introduced to the séance by Dr Trench, a Swedenborgian scholar. Corbet is sceptical but curious. Trench has never been to any of Mrs Henderson's séances before and has argued 'that I could get more out of Emanuel Swedenborg than out of any séance'. His function is to introduce Corbet while he is curious, in addition, about talk of a hostile spirit. Miss Mackenna, the secretary of the Dublin Spiritualists Association, of which Dr Trench is president, is open-minded. Sometimes she feels 'it is all coincidence and thought-transference', but at other times 'I feel like Job – you know the quotation – the hair of my head stands up. A spirit passes before my face.' These three figures are disinterested spectators, curious for knowledge. The remaining three sitters are looking for results. While the first three are represented as intelligent and sensitive, the latter three are caricatures. Abraham Johnson comes from Belfast man, a city Yeats associated with industrialism and materialism. Johnson is 'a minister of the Gospel' and he wishes to reach the spirit of Sankey and to be given his power as a preacher. Mrs Mallet is looking for advice from her dead husband as to whether she should open a tea-shop in Folkestone. Cornelius Patterson has come to find out about a new idea of heaven. He dislikes that of the Church and has heard that men can eat and drink in the after-life, 'I said to myself, "That is the place for Corney Patterson."'

The responses to the hostile spirit vary. Abraham Johnson and Mrs Mallet are convinced of its evil, Johnson advocating exorcism. Dr Trench, however, offers a different definition:

The spirits are people like ourselves, we treat them as our guests and protect them from discourtesy and violence, and every exorcism is a curse or a threatened curse. We do not admit that there are evil spirits. Some spirits are earthbound . . . .

Such spirits are compelled to repeat the pain and suffering of their lives:

In vain do we write *requiescat in pace* upon the tomb, for they must suffer, . . . until God gives peace. Such spirits do not often come to séances unless those séances are held in houses where those spirits lived, or where the event took place. The spirit which speaks those incomprehensible words and does not answer when spoken to is of such a nature. The more patient we are, the more quickly will it pass out of its passion and its remorse.

Parallel to this and without apparent awareness of any connection, the doctor and Corbet discuss Swift. This was a house where Stella came often. There are words etched in the window-pane which Corbet recognises as the words of a poem Stella had written to Swift. The doctor's words echo the tone of Swift's: 'A tragic life: Bolingbroke, Harley, Ormonde, all those great Ministers that were his friends, banished and broken.' Corbet sees a deeper underlying tragedy: 'His ideal order was the Roman Senate, his ideal men Brutus and Cato. Such an order and such men had seemed possible once more, but the movement passed and he foresaw the ruin to come . . . .' This ruin is paralleled in the condition of the house, once set in the country, now a decaying suburban lodging-house.

Mrs Henderson, the medium, begins the séance with a hymn. Her control is Lulu, 'a dear little girl . . . who died when she was five or six years old'. The incongruity between even the name 'Lulu' and the haunted figure of Swift is startling. Her baby-talk is abruptly broken into by the more eloquent rage of Swift:

> That bad man, that bad old man in the corner, they have let him come back. Lulu is going to scream. O . . . O . . . . (*In a man's voice*) How dare you write to her? How dare you ask if we were married? How dare you question her?

The 'horrible play' begins as Dr Trench observes, 'A soul in its agony – it cannot see us or hear us.' The medium and the sitters become irrelevant. They are merely the vehicles through which we see Swift. Corbet had conveniently defined the work of the medium: ' A state of somnambulism and voices coming through her lips that purport to be those of dead persons?' Mrs Henderson, as the Guardian of the Well in *At the Hawk's Well*, becomes an unconscious vessel of inspiration.

The 'horrible play' which Swift is forced to perform begins with his relationship with Vanessa and brings to the surface the twin questions of his madness and his loathing of the flesh. The story which Yeats follows tells of Swift's 'sending his servant out to fetch him a woman, and dismissing that servant when he woke to find a black woman at his side' (Introduction to *The Words upon the Window-Pane*). Yeats sees Swift as an intensely passionate figure. Hence he argues that there is always a third person present in Swift's meetings with Stella. For Yeats this corroborates the theory of Swift's dread of madness: 'he might well have been driven to consorting with the nameless women of the streets'. Of Swift's relationship with Vanessa Yeats tells us, 'that excited blue-stocking bores me'. In the play Swift's response to Vanessa reveals his ideal standard of behaviour. Vanessa, taught to think 'as Cato or Brutus would', now behaves 'like some common slut with her ear against the keyhole'. Yet Vanessa appears as a dominant force in the play. She threatens, even terrifies, Swift with her arguments:

> Give me both your hands. I will put them upon my breast. O it is white – white as the gambler's dice – white ivory dice. Think of the uncertainty. Perhaps a mad child – perhaps a rascal – perhaps a knave – perhaps not, Jonathan. The dice of the intellect are loaded, but I am the common ivory dice.

As I have pointed out, David Clark in his study suggests that Swift may have erred in refusing to take this gamble. There is, however, another way of looking at Swift's dilemma and that is to draw a parallel with the action of *The Only Jealousy of Emer*, where Fand offers Cuchulain the temptation of annihilating oblivion. Although Fand is supernatural and Vanessa firmly rooted to the earth, both offer the hero an escape and the destruction of an integrity. Swift's integrity, his role, is his self-divided nature, his suffering, his later madness and poverty. By denying sex he intensifies and perhaps perverts its strength: 'My God, do you think it was easy? I was a man of strong passions and I had sworn never to marry.' Vanessa's parting words operate as a curse:

> no man in Ireland is so passionate. That is why you need me, that is why you need children, nobody has greater need. You are growing old. An old man without children is very solitary. Even his friends, men as old as he, turn away, they turn towards the young, their children. . . . They cannot endure an old man like themselves. . . . a few years if you turn away will make you an old miserable childless man.

There is a deep horror in Swift's response: 'O God, hear the prayer of Jonathan Swift, that afflicted man, and grant that he may leave to posterity nothing but his intellect that came to him from Heaven.'

On this scene of intense suffering the door is locked. The sense of being trapped is intensified by the play's technique. Only a voice remains. There is no silencing it. Swift is trapped. Is it with Vanessa, or is it with himself? It seems to me that Swift is trapped by that part of himself represented by Vanessa, with his loathed humanity, his own 'blood-sodden heart': 'My God, I am left alone with my enemy. Who locked the door, who locked me in with my enemy?' Swift's revelation of the human condition as utterly detestable, filthy, brutal and grotesque gains its depth by his recognition of his own identity with it. In *Gulliver's Travels* Swift's horror is always a matter of self-recognition. Gulliver's encounter with the female Yahoo seems pertinent to Yeats's play: 'For now I could no longer deny, that I was a real Yahoo in every limb and feature, since the females had a natural propensity to me as one of their own species.'[56] On his return to England Gulliver's horror is expressed through the primary sense of smell:

> And when I began to consider, that by copulating with one of the Yahoo species, I had become a parent of more, it struck me with the utmost shame, confusion and horror . . . . I could not endure my wife or children in my presence, the very smell of them was intolerable.[57]

Such Swiftean disgust at life has its fullest expression, in Yeats's work, in *Purgatory*.

The second 'act' of Swift's 'horrible play' concerns Stella. The sitters notice a change in the atmosphere of the room which brings to the suffering Swift a healing power, a consolation. Stella is his ideal. He has made her so:

> With what scorn you speak of the common lot of women. . . . It is the thought of the great Chrysostom who wrote in a famous passage that women loved according to the soul, loved as the saints can love, keep their beauty longer, have greater happiness than women loved according to the flesh. That thought has comforted me, but it is a terrible thing to be responsible for another's happiness.

Swift's faith is fractured: 'There are moments when I doubt . . . .' We recall Yeats's comments in his Introduction: 'It seems certain that Swift loved her though he called it by some other name, and she him, and that it was platonic love' (*VPl*, p. 966). Stella's poem, etched in the window-pane, to which Swift now turns, speaks of rational affection, of balance, harmony and control. Stella is the opposite of Vanessa with her ivory dice. The poem, as Torchiana points out,[58] bears a direct relationship to Swift's theory of civilisation:

> You taught how I might youth prolong
> By knowing what is right and wrong;
> How from my heart to bring supplies
> Of lustre to my failing eyes;
> How soon a beauteous mind repairs
> The loss of chang'd or falling hairs,
> How wit and virtue from within
> Can spread a smoothness o'er the skin.

Stella seems an antidote to the loneliness Vanessa threatened:

> Late dying you may cast a shred
> Of that rich mantle o'er my head;
> To bear with dignity my sorrow,
> One day alone, then die tomorrow.

But Stella does not live to close his eyes. In the end Swift is old, miserable, mad and deserted.

The third 'act' of Yeats's play breaks through the naturalistic and common-place world of the séance. Mrs Henderson tells Corbet that just as she woke up she saw that 'His clothes were dirty, his face covered with boils. Some disease had made one of his eyes swell up, it stood out from his face like a hen's egg.' Physical appearance finally reflects Swift's vision of life as repulsive and horrific. But his voice remains eloquent in its expression of loss: 'Five great Ministers that were my friends are gone, ten great Ministers that were my friends are gone. I have not fingers enough to count the great Ministers that were my friends and that are gone.' His words catch up into themselves the words of Dr Trench at the beginning of the play. The final words, 'Perish the day on which I was born', frightening as they break unbidden through the lips of Mrs Henderson, leave us with Swift's Vision of Evil. Swift expresses an absolute integrity which may be summed up as one of loss. He experiences the dark side of tragic vision and, as in 'The Cold Heaven', is sent 'Out naked on the roads as the books say, and stricken / By the injustice of the skies for punishment' (*CP*, p. 140).

I conclude this chapter with an exploration of *Purgatory* (*CPl*, pp. 681–9). Whatever our feelings about the merits of this play, I do not think we can escape seeing it as an inferno as much as a purgatory. We cannot escape seeing in it an evil which thwarts and destroys at every turn. F. A. Lucas in his magnificently prejudiced discussion of Yeats's drama comments,

> This has been called Yeats's finest play. It would be terrible if that were true. . . . And further, passionately sincere though Yeats was in his regret for the aristocratic civilisation of the past, we may still wonder whether this piece about a brutal old pedlar who in youth murders his father, and in age his son, is itself very civilised.[59]

Helen Vendler takes a slightly less limited view of the play, but, while relating it to *The Dreaming of the Bones*, she sees it as a deterioration:

> Again we have a troubled spirit compulsively repeating events out of the past, and again we have the spectator who is somehow involved in the spirit's action. But in the twenty-two years which intervened between the composition of the two plays, Yeats's mood changed decisively, and I would say for the worse.[60]

Peter Ure, a more sympathetic critic, also comments on the relationship between these two plays:

> Both plays are concerned with the remorse of the dead, and in the earlier one there is a hint that the living, the 'others' who suffer the consequences of the crimes of the dead, may help them. In *The Dreaming of the Bones* the soldier's forgiveness might have assuaged the torment of Diarmuid and Dervogilla. The whole subject of *Purgatory* is such an assuagement . . . .[61]

It is however an abortive attempt. Ure comments on the fact that in the one play the intervention would be pardon, while in the latter it is murder. This 'affords a measure of the difference between the finished, melancholy and somewhat self-conscious beauty of *The Dreaming of the Bones* and the squalor, sexuality and violence of *Purgatory*'.[62]

Purgatory is graced by no musicians' chorus, yet the play is close in form and impact to the earlier dance plays. As in them, a landscape is created in the mind's eye. This landscape is stark: a ruined house and a stunted tree are all that we are given. Vision is embodied entirely through the words of the Old Man. In his anger and disgust he looks forward to the Old Man in *The Death of Cuchulain* – 'I spit! I spit! I spit!' (*CPl*, p. 694), – and back to the persona in 'A Dialogue of Self and Soul' (*CP*, pp. 265–7), 'A blind man battering blind men'. But Self in that poem is able to forgive himself and his world:

> When such as I cast out remorse
> So great a sweetness flows into the breast
> We must laugh and we must sing,
> We are blest by everything,
> Everything we look upon is blest.

The impossibility of forgiveness lies at the centre of *Purgatory*. It seems to me that there are two themes operating together perhaps uneasily. One theme is Ireland and its house devastated by civil war and petty strife which has attacked both good and bad with indifference. The other is the theme of disgust, disgust at the human race and the paradoxical act of love which engenders it. The Old Man puts a house before us – 'Study that house' – and the play compels us to see it first as Ireland, eroded from its past glory, and then as Crazy Jane's house in the poem 'Crazy Jane on God' (*CP*, pp. 293–4). My argument is that in this play Yeats puts before us all that he can of his Vision of Evil. In 'A Dialogue of Self and Soul' Yeats's disgust is tempered with mercy and renewal. For Crazy Jane love not only destroys but also redeems us. Except in so far as the Old Man's prayer at the end implies the faintest possibility of release, Yeats offers no glimmer of light here.

Even the imagined glory of the house's past is besmirched. The Old Man begins with the tree:

> I saw it fifty years ago
> Before the thunderbolt had riven it,
> Green leaves, ripe leaves, leaves thick as butter,
> Fat, greasy life.

This is not the chestnut tree of 'Among School Children'. The implication is that, when the mother married her stable groom the richness of the house had already grown over-ripe. It is a long time since 'Great people lived and died in this house'. If we take this play as a disgusted taunt at modern Ireland we have to remember that the Old Man is mixed of two bloods and that when he exclaims,

> to kill a house
> Where great men grew up, married, died,
> I here declare a capital offence

his rage also tells on himself. The Old Man is unable to see, with Crazy Jane in 'Crazy Jane Talks with the Bishop' (*CP*, pp. 294–5), that 'Fair and foul are near of kin, / And fair needs foul', or that

> Love has pitched his mansion in
> The place of excrement;
> For nothing can be sole or whole
> That has not been rent.

It is, I feel, the Old Man who suffers purgatory. It is he who is compelled to relive the sin of his own begetting. He is immersed in 'the frog-spawn of a blind man's ditch' ('A Dialogue of Self and Soul', *CP*, p. 267), just as his son is born in degradation, 'A bastard that a pedlar got / Upon a tinker's daughter in a ditch'. Yet neither murder of the father who begot him, nor of the son whom he begot, can free him 'from the crime of being born' ('Consolation', *CP*, p. 310). He is compelled to see it again and again:

> Listen to the hoof-beats! Listen! Listen! . . .

> She has gone down to open the door.
> This night she is no better than her man
> And does not mind that he is half-drunk,
> She is mad about him.

The Old Man appeals, 'Do not let him touch you!' He is compelled, as an unwilling voyeur, to watch over the squalid pleasure of their marriage-bed:

> there's a problem: she must live
> Through everything in exact detail,
> Driven to it by remorse, and yet
> Can she renew the sexual act
> And find no pleasure in it, and if not,
> If pleasure and remorse must both be there,
> Which is the greater?

Peter Ure comments,

> The remorseful spirit must, in order to be free of it, repeat, explore, or dream through the crime which it committed during life; but in this case the renewal of the act, because of the nature of the act, renews the self-degrading pleasure that accompanied it. Thus the very consequence from which release is sought – self-degradation – is entailed upon the mother's spirit each time she lives through her transgression.[63]

I should argue that it is equally entailed on her son. Crazy Jane, of course, reveals the sexual act in another light:

> Before their eyes a house
> That from childhood stood
> Uninhabited, ruinous,
> Suddenly lit up
> From door to top:
> *All things remain in God.*
> > (*CP*, p. 294)

It could have been the same house. *Purgatory* presents distorted and perverted the rage that Yeats perceives as noble in Oedipus and as an instrument for truth in 'An Acre of Grass'.

Swift and the Old Man of *Purgatory* articulate a nightmare vision of humanity, society and history. Both through the panoramic vision of an ever-repeating historical tragedy and within the personal life, Yeats presents what can with conviction be called a Vision of Evil. We may see in Yeats, as with his imagined Dante, that creation which leaps up ecstatically like Colonus's 'horses of the sea, white horses' (*CP*, p. 246; *CPl*, p. 544) is also from terror. But standing back to back with the visions presented in *The Words upon the Window-Pane* and in *Purgatory* we have Sophocles' *Oedipus at Colonus* (*CPl*, pp. 521–75), which balances hatred with love. In the song 'Endure what life . . .' (*CP*, p. 255; *CPl*, p. 561) Yeats concertinas images from the play into the one image of the love-act, which engenders birth, death, sin and the whole Theban cycle of tragedy:

> Even from that delight memory treasures so,
> Death, despair, division of families, all entanglements
>   of mankind grow,
> As that old wandering beggar and these God-hated children
>   know.

The stanza reveals love both as delight and despair. The 'long echoing street' of the next stanza carries us back into the streets of history, but forward as well. A bridal song remains the central image of joy:

> In the long echoing street the laughing dancers throng,
> The bride is carried to the bridegroom's chamber through
>   torchlight and tumultuous song;
> I celebrate the silent kiss that ends short life or long.

Love, like Oedipus's death, his miraculous descent into the earth, sets us free from division and the whirling movement of the gyres. The first two lines of the final stanza are belied by the last line. For the tragic hero's 'gay goodnight' is his victory in the face of death:

> Never to have lived is best, ancient writers say;
> Never to have drawn the breath of life, never to
>   have looked into the eye of day . . . .

So the Old Man in *Purgatory* would say, but, just as Self in 'A Dialogue of Self and Soul' rejects his death-wish and finds, like Oedipus, that he is blessed and can bless, so here the second best is best. After laughter and song, 'a gay goodnight and quickly turn away'.

Conclusion: The Death of the Hero

In *On the Boiler* Yeats writes,

> The arts are all the bridal chambers of joy. No tragedy is legitimate unless it leads some great character to his final joy. Polonius may go out wretchedly, but I can hear the dance music in 'Absent thee from felicity awhile', or in Hamlet's speech over the dead Ophelia, and what of Cleopatra's last farewells, Lear's rage under the lightning, Oedipus sinking down at the story's end into an earth 'riven' by love? Some Frenchman has said that farce is the struggle against a ridiculous object, comedy against a movable object, tragedy against an immovable; and because the will, or energy, is greatest in tragedy, tragedy is the more noble; but I add that 'will or energy is eternal delight', and when its limit is reached it may become a pure, aimless joy, though the man, the shade, still mourns his lost object.   (*E*, pp. 448–9)

This definition of tragic joy and the movement of the tragic process through will and energy to a joy pure and aimless recapitulates much of what Yeats has written of tragedy. Indeed, as I have already suggested, the 1904 essay 'First Principles' (*E*, pp. 141–63), establishes that the tragic artist transforms mere sorrow into an eternal gesture of life, life's delighted expense of energy. In 'Hodos Chameliontis', *Autobiographies* offers the clearest exposition of the man who 'still mourns his lost object' while accepting the loss with joy (pp. 272–3). 'The Tragic Theatre' defines Yeats's response to and evocation of tragic ecstasy in which we climb beyond purgatory (*E&I*, p. 238), just as, in 'A General Introduction for my Work', we are taken through 'aboriginal ice' towards vision (*E&I*, p. 599). What must be stressed here is the element of the unique and strange, matter for

137

wonder, which accompanies this final aimless and hence, in a way, passive joy. We can of course relate this to the wisdom of the fool in Yeats's cycle of the phases of the moon, and indeed this is how Skene perceives Cuchulain in the final play.[1] What characterises this moment of tragic recognition, which is also, I argue, a moment of transfiguration or transformation, is not simply disintegration of order, though this must be a part of it – 'the burning roof and tower' (*CP* p. 241) – but complete vision, the eye widening on a landscape in which strange becomes familiar and familiar strange. As I suggested earlier, Yeats's evocation of tragic ecstasy is compounded both of extravagance and sterility, what I attempted to define as a triumphant penury or pessimistic ecstasy. Throughout Yeats's career tragic joy is somehow 'A most astonishing thing' (*CP*, p. 340). Deirdre's triumphant death becomes the entry to a 'secret wilderness of love', 'A high, grey cairn' (*CPl*, p. 202). In the poem 'Demon and Beast' Anthony's joy is expressed as sweetness:

> O what a sweetness strayed
> Through barren Thebaid . . . .
> (*CP*, p. 210)

And, as Yeats suggests in the quotation with which I opened this conclusion, Shakespeare's heroes and heroines are, in their final moments, brought to a quiet gaiety, even to gentleness. The last moments of tragedy characteristically descend from a climax of pain or conflict into exhaustion. Tragedy dissipates itself, if you like, into the air, into a breath: 'Thou'lt come no more, / Never, never, never, never, never' (*King Lear*, V, iii).

In Yeats's view, as we have seen, tragedy is not a choice but a necessity; it is his explanation of the world. We have traced a path through Yeats's dance plays and their evocation of the moment of tragic recognition and their use of a characteristic landscape of barren rock and stunted tree to evoke this moment. We have explored *A Vision* and the tragic universe in which progress is replaced by endless repetition both in the historical cycle and in the individual life. Man is always confronted by his opposite; is doomed to lose what he loves; is thwarted and must finally encounter death. Yet even beyond this point there is no eternal rest, for the cycle starts again. In such a universe joy is a paradoxical phenomenon, an instant in which eternity may be glimpsed, a timeless moment. We have discussed Yeats's Vision of Evil and its part in his tragic vision together with his response to Christianity and the implications of his system for the judgement of good and evil, innocence and responsibility. Throughout we have seen Yeats confront opposite with opposite, flesh with spirit, love with hate, torturer with tortured, light with dark. Over all has lain the sense of a disintegrating order and the threat, or promise, of reversal, the anarchic dawn of a new age. Now in conclusion we turn to Cuchulain, the hero's last battle and his response to death in *The Death of Cuchulain*. We must, I argue, explore this play in the light of Yeats's comments in *On the Boiler*: 'No tragedy is legitimate unless it leads some great character to his final joy (*E*, p. 449). Yeats's evocation of Cuchulain must stand or fall by this criterion.

Peter Ure sums up one dominant critical response to this play when he rejects F. A. C. Wilson's verdict that 'the play, a play of rejoicing, centres about transfiguration':[2] 'This misrepresents the structure of the play in which I see not transfiguration, and certainly not rejoicing – though there is a kind of grim joy in it – but the death of the hero seen as the final irony of fate.'[3] Ure does not, however, explain just how we are to distinguish 'rejoicing' from 'a kind of grim joy'. Harold Bloom also rejects Wilson's verdict on the play and he argues,

> Helen Vendler precisely renders the play's tone when she says that weariness and indifference, rather than tragic joy, come nearer its note. Cuchulain, at the end, passes from quiet disgust through exhaustion to a state of simply not caring.[4]

Both Ure and Bloom place a great deal of significance on one of Cuchulain's lines: 'Twelve pennies! What better reason for killing a man?' Ure remarks of Cuchulain that this is 'almost his last comment on the heroic adventure, and a total denial of all its glorious rationale'.[5] He concludes, 'This is an acceptance, but it is not a transfiguration.'[6] Bloom comments that here 'bitterness demeans the hero',[7] although he adds this is but momentary. Bloom sees Yeats's intentions in this play as entirely destructive and negative: 'Yeats intends a final destruction of any myth of the hero, his own included. Cuchulain must die badly, and for no purpose and no result, die as evidence of the end coming to no end.'[8] But he feels that Yeats's intentions are subverted by his hero even though he 'wished to yield the hero's dignity to the tides of destruction'[9] and even though the play's *dénouement*, the Blind Man groping for the hero's throat, is 'Yeats's brutal and sordid triumph over the enchantment of heroism'.[10]

Two critical problems confront us with this play: the question of what were Yeats's intentions and the problem of irony. The two are, I should argue, linked. The ironies are reasonably easy to locate. They centre around Eithne Inguba's unwilling betrayal of Cuchulain, his refusal to accept her word when she tells the truth, and Aoife's appearance as avenger, but an avenger who is thwarted by the despicable Blind Man. Of the first irony, Ure comments that Cuchulain goes to his death without realising that it will be his death. He is full of 'reckless energy . . . seeking glory in a fight against the odds and behaving with generous forbearance to the woman whom he thinks has tried to bring about his death'.[11] Ure argues that Yeats's Cuchulain differs from the protagonist of his main source, Lady Gregory's *Cuchulain of Muirthemne*, in that he does not knowingly go out to die:

> The irony, plain to be seen by the audience, derives from the tangle of misunderstandings that is netted about these fine attitudes and drags the hero down. Because his eyes are dazzled by the vision of heroic strife, he cannot recognise the goddess of death standing before him, who makes a doom out of the adventure. Nor can he recognise the faithfulness of Eithne. . . . Cuchulain's end is being determined by his own desire and by his fixed interpretation of the hero's role.[12]

This last sentence reminds us clearly of the trap in which Cuchulain is caught in *On Baile's Strand*. Ure argues that at the end of the play's first part, Yeats, despite showing the hero to be trapped in misunderstanding, nevertheless intends Cuchulain to astound us 'with his majesty'. But, he asks, when we come to the second part of the play, 'What is done to this majesty?'[13] Ure talks of a Cuchulain 'whose voice and rhythms have stilled and melted into the weakness and confusion of the dying'.[14] For Ure, Aoife's presence is the most significant feature of this part of the play and this leads to 'a resounding irony'.[15] The dialogue between Aoife and Cuchulain slowly shapes a pattern in which the tragedies of Baile's strand and the hawk's well are remembered. The old story of love mixed with hatred, frustration and tragic error builds up towards what is plainly its one right ending – that Aoife should at last revenge upon his father the death of Conlaoch.[16]

Clearly Ure feels that Cuchulain's 'true death' is thwarted and that he meets at the hands of the Blind Man mere 'mass death'.[17] Just why revenge 'would have meaningfully completed work, life and death'[18] I am not sure. On the contrary, I feel that the irony of Cuchulain's death is also the most fitting end for this hero, as I shall show in my discussion of the play. To the list of ironies Harold Bloom adds perceptively that 'The largest irony of *The Death of Cuchulain* is that only the hero has grown indifferent.'[19] Eithne is passionate in her wish to protect Cuchulain; Aoife is passionate in her desire for revenge; the Blind Man is hardly indifferent – to gain, at any rate.

But what of Yeats's intentions in this play? What do these ironies mean? Is Yeats really intent on destroying the hero and his dignity? The first thing to remember here is that the play is part of a cycle. The Old Man of the prologue announces that *The Death of Cuchulain (CPl, pp. 693–705)* is 'the last of a series of plays which has for theme his life and death. I have been selected because I am out of fashion and out of date like the antiquated romantic stuff the thing is made of.' As we shall see, the prologue is deliberately aggressive and jarring. We are forced to recall a remark from Yeats's Introduction to *Fighting the Waves*: 'I would have attempted the Battle of the Fords and The Death of Cuchulain had not the mood of Ireland changed' (*VPl*, p. 568). Yeats's play takes fully into account that change of mood and the poet's own bitter disillusion. But the prologue's reference to a series of plays should also make us look at this play in the context of the other Cuchulain plays. The first thing to say of this is that the final play with all its irony is quite in keeping with the treatment of Cuchulain in earlier plays. He is constantly shown as thwarted, misled, bewitched by the Shape-Changers. His encounters have been directed as much against the supernatural as against any tangible enemy. He is at war with himself as well as with a hostile twentieth-century environment. Each play, as I have suggested, is concerned with a potential death-encounter.

His destiny and death, which are finally identical, are Cuchulain's true opponents throughout Yeats's cycle.

Another way in which Yeats's intentions in this play may be clarified is through an examination of some of his sources. The foremost of these is Lady Gregory's *Cuchulain of Muirthemne*. In this version Cuchulain does realise the trick that has been played on him, but he still goes out to death: 'my luck has turned against me, and my life is near its end, and I will not come back alive this time from facing the men of Ireland. . . . And it is not now I will begin to draw back . . . for a great name outlasts life.'[20] Lady Gregory describes Cuchulain's final movements:

> Then he gathered up his bowels into his body, and he went down to the lake. He drank a drink, and he washed himself, and he turned back again to his death, and he called to his enemies to come and meet him.

> There was a pillar-stone west of the lake . . . and he tied himself to it with his breast-belt, the way he would not meet his death lying down, but would meet it standing up.[21]

In this version neither Aoife nor Blind Man is present. Emer laments over the head of Cuchulain, a lament which Yeats will transform into her dance at the play's end: 'And Emer took the head of Cuchulain in her hands, and she washed it clean, and put a silk cloth about it.'[22] She cries 'Ochone! . . . it is good the beauty of this head was, though it is low this day.'[23] Lady Gregory's chronicle ends with this note, a note which I think Yeats echoes both in the play and in the poem 'Cuchulain Comforted': 'But the three times fifty queens that loved Cuchulain saw him appear in his Druid chariot, going through Emain Macha; and they could hear him singing the music of the Sidhe.'[24]

Yeats's Blind Man is the most significant addition to this tale, but, though he is Yeats's own creation, his use here is not entirely without precedent. The source for this incident tends to be overlooked. In Chapter 1 I drew brief attention to it in discussing Yeats's response to Ferguson's 'Congal':[25]

> It is the story of the death in the seventh century, at the battle of Moyra (or Moira) of Congal Claen. Congal was a heathen;

his enemy, the arch-King Ardrigh, was a Christian. This war was the sunset of Irish heathendom.[26]

Yeats paraphrases the march of Congal and his army across Ireland, demons prophesying their destruction; but, 'Defying heaven and hell, on march the heathen hosts'.[27] Yeats pauses at their encounter with 'the Washer of the Ford' – a grey hag 'to knees in the river, washing the heads, and the bodies of men'.[28] Congal questions her. She is of the Tuath de Danaan, her bed 'in the middle of the shell-heaped Cairn of Maev',[29] high up on Knocknarea. She is steeped in carnage, washing the heads of those whom Congal is even now leading to death:

> 'And this', the Fury said,
> Uplifting by the clotted locks what seemed a dead man's
> head,
> 'Is thine head, O Congal!'[30]

As with Cuchulain, Congal's host ignore all portents. Yeats continues,

> Still on they go, these indomitable pagans. Surely nothing will resist their onset. Will they not even shake the throne of God in their sublime audacity? No; Congal when he has accomplished deeds of marvellous valour is slain by the hand of an idiot boy who carries a sickle for sword, and the lid of a cauldron for shield. Ah, strange irony of the Celt![31]

Cuchulain, the last hero, faces the materialist and anti-heroic world just as Congal, the last heathen, faces the new Christian world. Congal meets his death at the hands of an idiot, Cuchulain at the hands of a blind man. Both deaths are ironic; yet we can see that Yeats considers this final twisting of the knife characteristic of the Celtic imagination. Instances of such irony abound in Yeats's work and indeed are intrinsic to his characteristic portrayal of the heroic. Swift ends in madness, Parnell in disgrace amid the rabble who had adored him. The hero is torn down by the low and base, by his opposite. It is the response to death which matters.

Yeats's play uses some techniques from the dance plays, but it is really a new form of presentation. The play is framed by a prologue of invective prose at the beginning, and a dance and a song at the close. But the song mirrors something of the tone of the opening. Prologue and song provide a context in which to view Cuchulain's final encounter. The strangeness of the heroic world is emphasised by the play's shift from the contemporary to the mythological past. The twentieth-century audience watch Cuchulain, but one feels that, when Cuchulain senses the Blind Man's hands upon his body, he is looking out from the past into our own present. Helen Vendler writes harshly of the prologue. The Old Man's speech is 'shrill frenzy'. His attack on his times is 'giving up on society altogether', she argues – 'a much more tenable position for a lyric poet than a dramatist'.[32] This seems to me strange, for the Old Man confronts and attacks rather than retreats from what he regards as inimical. Besides which, he is obviously deliberately exaggerated. Vendler concludes of the stagecraft involved in the dance, 'Once a dramatist reaches a point where he thinks that "no wood carving can look as well as a parallelogram of painted wood" he is no longer talking to an audience.'[33]

This judgement is largely a question of subjective taste. The significant question to ask here is whether or not the play remains intelligible to the audience. From this point of view the Old Man's Prologue is essential, because, with all its angry contempt, it also explains the dance at the play's end:

> I promise a dance. I wanted a dance because where there are no words there is less to spoil. Emer must dance, there must be severed heads – I am old, I belong to mythology – severed heads for her to dance before. I had thought to have had those heads carved, but no, if the dancer can dance properly no wood-carving can look as well as a parallelogram of painted wood.

Skene comments on Yeats's apparent abandonment of lyric – 'where there are no words there is less to spoil' – that

> This may seem to be a curious position for a poetic playwright to take. The reference is to the musical part of drama, or at least to that ritual portion that tends towards music. On the stage, Yeats has found that music and dance merge more successfully than music and lyric.[34]

Just as words may distract, so carven heads may distract from the dance which Yeats sees as central to the play. Yeats's Old Man seeks a fit dancer for his play: 'I could have got such a dancer once, but she has gone; the tragi-comedian dancer, the tragic dancer, upon the same neck love and loathing, life and death.'[35] We recall Yeats's Introduction to *Certain Noble Plays of Japan*, where he describes a dance as 'the tragic image which has stirred my imagination' (*E&I*, p. 224), and Fand's dance in *Fighting the Waves*. From this dance, the Old Man tells us, nothing is to distract. The use of parallelograms should be seen in this context, as an extension of Yeats's anti-naturalist stage-craft. The Old Man's conclusion contrasts the image of tragedy, the dancer who balances on the one neck life, death, love and hatred, with Degas's dancers:

> I spit three times. I spit upon the dancers painted by Degas. I spit upon their short bodices, their stiff stays, their toes whereon they spin like peg-tops, above all upon that chamber-maid face. They might have looked timeless . . . . I spit! I spit! I spit!

Yeats's tragic dance is to suggest the timeless, the archetypal, the eternal gesture which stands free from 'that old maid history'.

With the prologue completed, the curtain rises on a bare stage. Eithne Inguba enters calling, 'Cuchulain! Cuchulain!' followed by the hero himself. Eithne immediately plunges into the speech which betrays both her own loyalty and Cuchulain's life: 'The scene is set and you must out and fight.' When Eithne realises that 'Maeve put me in a trance' and when Cuchulain answers her question, 'Who among the gods of the air and upper air / Has a bird's head?', much is made of the irony of this betrayal, as we have seen. But beneath these ironies of witch-craft, confusion and misunderstanding there is a sense of the inevitable working of destiny: 'The scene is set'. This is the true end for Cuchulain. Cuchulain's refusal to believe Eithne, his suggestion that she may want 'a younger man, a friendlier man' finds its fullest expression in terms of the heroic code:

> You thought that if you changed I'd kill you for it,
> When everything sublunary must change,

> And if I have not changed that goes to prove
> That I am monstrous.[36]

This, rather than Cuchulain's later remarks about the price of a
man's head, is where we should ask about the hero's rejection of
the heroic code. For, though Cuchulain will not abandon that
code, he talks of it as monstrous, grotesque, ugly; 'everything
sublunary must change' just as in 'Easter 1916' the living change
'Minute by minute' (*CP*, p. 204), as the clouds move in the sky,
while the dead stone of the fanatical heart lies at the centre,
unmoved by the stream of life. Cuchulain's response to Eithne,
which calls forth her rebuke, 'You're not the man I loved, / That
violent man forgave no treachery', reveals the hero as Yeats
wished him to appear in *On Baile's Strand*. Cuchulain's personality, there, was to express a quality 'hard, repellent yet allur-
ing'. Cuchulain was to be seen as the fool, 'wandering passive,
houseless and almost loveless' (*L*, p. 425). I should argue that
Cuchulain as he is presented in this final play is Yeats's most
successful evocation of the hero. Cuchulain is not shrouded or
dwarfed by the landscape. He is colder, finer and more articulate
than in *On Baile's Strand* or other plays in the cycle. Finally, as
this section of the play closes, Eithne remarks,

> I might have peace that know
> The Morrigu, the woman like a crow,
> Stands to my defence and cannot lie,
> But that Cuchulain is about to die.

The Morrigu suggests the inevitability of Cuchulain's death.
Eithne is an unwilling vehicle for destiny or fate, a fate which is
also independent of Maeve's deceit.

In the second section of the play lights rise on a stage bare of
people but dominated by a pillar-stone. Cuchulain, now fatally
wounded, enters and tries to tie himself to the stone, but he
cannot. Aoife, 'white-haired', an astonishing turnabout for a
heroic tale, now enters. She helps to fasten him to the stone,
which is to say that she helps him to fulfil his heroic role, to die
upright. As already discussed, much is made of Aoife's heroic
equality with Cuchulain. Cuchulain acknowledges, 'You have a
right to kill me', and, when Aoife boasts,

> The grey of Macha, that great horse of yours
> Killed in the battle, came out of the pool
> As though it were alive, and went three times
> In a great circle round you and that stone,
> Then leaped into the pool; and not a man
> Of all that terrified army dare approach,
> But I approach

Cuchulain repeats, 'Because you have the right.' But Cuchulain is already dying and his conversation with Aoife is part of that journey into death, a reliving of the past.

Aoife's purpose is thwarted, for it is the Blind Man's 'lucky day'. Cuchulain has recalled the slaying of his son, and now the Blind Man recalls, 'I stood between a Fool and the sea at Baile's strand / When you went mad.' There, in fear of strength, but indifferent to heroic *virtus*, the Blind Man saw to his own survival and gain. Now fear is removed. Cuchulain is wound about with 'Some womanish stuff'. The Blind Man evokes from the hero the cry, 'Twelve pennies! What better reason for killing a man?' Cuchulain, it seems to me, here recognises the irony of death and final victory of the hostile, mean and unheroic world. Yeats's own and the Old Man's voices break through. The prophecy of the Red Man in *The Green Helmet* is fulfilled. The day has come 'When heart and mind shall darken that the weak may end the strong' (*CPl*, p. 243). The Blind Man is sordid and revolting. His hands have to grope to find Cuchulain's neck. His actions are a form of sacrilege. Cuchulain asks, 'You have a knife, but have you sharpened it?' – to which the Blind Man replies, echoing the degraded world of *Purgatory*, 'I keep it sharp because it cuts my food.' But Cuchulain's journey, begun with Aoife, continues in indifference to the mere means of execution:

> There floats out there
> The shape that I shall take when I am dead,
> My soul's first shape, a soft feathery shape,
> And is not that a strange shape for the soul
> Of a great fighting-man?

The Blind man's, 'Are you ready Cuchulain!' and his actions, which Skene likens to 'the darkness creeping over the sun during

an eclipse',[37] have become irrelevant as Cuchulain continues on
his journey towards vision: 'I say it is about to sing.' Bloom
comments, 'The moment is worth the play', and sees this as the
welling-up of a deeper imagination than that which inspires the
sordid triumph of the Blind Man.[38] Yet strangely this moment is
not, for him, a 'transfiguration'.[39] Surely Cuchulain's discovery
of himself as 'a soft feathery shape', surely the transformation of
the 'great fighting-man' into the soul with the throat of a bird,
must be defined as a transfiguration, and, though we may
quibble between the play's sense of 'rejoicing', the sense of 'grim
joy' and the sense of 'weary acceptance', I think we should
recognise in this moment a quietude that comes at the end of
struggle, a quietude close to Yeats's 'Pure, aimless joy' (*E*, pp.
448–9).

From this moment the play retreats from the tragic hero, first
to Emer's dance and finally to the song of the harlot. On
Cuchulain's death the stage darkens, and when the lights re-
appear the Morrigu dominates. She holds a parallelogram while six
others lie close by. She explains how the parallelograms represent first Cuchulain, then the six heroes who have given him
mortal wounds and died in the process. She concludes, 'I arranged the dance.' Harold Bloom comments,

> When the Morrigu, after Cuchulain is slain, implicitly claims
> the hero as her victim, it is unclear whether or not we are to
> believe her, but we do not anyway. He is self-slain as he was
> self-conceived, a sun in setting as he was in rising. We believe
> the Morrigu when she says: 'I arranged the dance' if this
> narrowly means Emer's dance of rage and mourning, which
> ends with the few faint bird notes of Cuchulain's comfort, his
> transformation in the death-between-lives. The Morrigu can
> provide context for Cuchulain, but not the wildness of uncon-
> ditioned freedom even of his exhausted will.[40]

Certainly Harold Bloom is right in noting Cuchulain's independence of his context, even, in a sense, of his death. The play's
ending (we could almost say its two endings) is summed up by
Ure when he says of the harlot's song, 'It leads away from the
event and generalises the emotion so that the curtain is folded
upon a distancing echo, the stage empty and ready to fade into
silence.'[41] But the Morrigu has dominated the play from the

beginning. She stands as the goddess not only of war, but also of death – 'The dead can hear me, and to the dead I speak' – and as such she fulfils something of the role of a personified destiny. Like the Instructors of *A Vision*, she presides over life and death, leading Cuchulain to his final and inevitable encounter.

There follows the dance of Emer, a dance which mingles rage, anger, adoration and triumph. Skene[42] relates this dance to the dance with severed head in *The King of the Great Clock Tower*, of which Yeats remarks that 'it is part of the old ritual of the year: the mother goddess and the slain god' (*VPl*, p. 1010), a reference which may remind us of 'Her Vision in the Wood' and 'Parnell's Funeral'. The dance, which culminates in triumph, is interrupted. Emer 'seems to hesitate between the head and what she hears. Then she stands motionless. There is silence, and in the silence a few faint bird notes.' Cuchulain's transformation is complete. This transformation is of course explored further in 'Cuchulain Comforted' and we might note briefly the alliance Yeats makes implicit between the Sidhe and the spirits of those between lives, an alliance between mythology and folklore and Yeats's own more esoteric system of reincarnation.

The final song comments ironically on this dance. It is not the most satisfactory of Yeats's songs and is one of the most ambiguous. Yeats here makes explicit the identity of the Easter Rising with the summoned presence of Cuchulain. An understanding of the song is, I feel, helped by reference to the poem 'Crazy Jane on the Mountain' (*CP*, pp. 390–1). Like Crazy Jane, the harlot contrasts sexual passion and physical beauty with a more paltry present:

> I adore those clever eyes,
> Those muscular bodies, but can get
> No grip upon their thighs.
> I meet those long pale faces,
> Hear their great horses, then
> Recall what centuries have passed
> Since they were living men.

This, as Ure also remarks,[43] recalls the technique of the Noh; it deliberately distances us from the heroic world, contrasting the ideal with the ordinary and time-bound. But the harlot for all her adoration cannot satisfy her passion with phantom presences from the past. She continues,

> That there are still some living
> That do my limbs unclothe,
> But that the flesh my flesh has gripped
> I both adore and loathe.

It seems that the harlot recalls a Golden Age without division, without the pain of desire and loathing, but we know from the prologue and its discussion of Emer's dance that the tragic image must be compounded of life and death, loathing and desire. The next stanza is more explicit. It begins with a question:

> Are those things that men adore and loathe
> Their sole reality?

The meaning of this question is not, I think, answered by either of the alternatives suggested by Skene: 'The question seems ambiguous. Does it mean: "Is material existence the sole reality?" Or does it mean: "Are those things that engage a man's emotions his sole reality?"'[44] The second alternative is closer to the truth, but, I feel that what is at issue here is the question of joy. As in 'Vacillation' (*CP*, p. 282) the poet asks the question, 'If we are caught between desire and the exhaustion of desire, between death and remorse, between love and loathing, can joy exist?' The song continues,

> What stood in the Post Office
> With Pearse and Connolly?
> What comes out of the mountain
> Where men first shed their blood?
> Who thought Cuchulain till it seemed
> He stood where they had stood?

There is a grim sense of joy here, a sense of primeval power, a power which suggests recurrence, the re-enactment of ritual slaughter. The lines also suggest encounter between opposites. Pearse and Connolly summon, as 'to the ancient winding stair' in 'A Dialogue of Self and Soul' (*CP*, p. 265), the desired and dreaded image of heroic strength, the image of sacrificial death, the image of Cuchulain tied to a stake to face his last enemies in dignity and unabashed. In this sense there is release from the perpetual swing between opposites, a release evoked by archetypal gesture and image. The cycles of history have been defeated by the summoning power of the imagination. This archetype dwarfs:

> No body like his body
> Has modern woman borne . . . .

The 'old man looking back on life / Imagines it in scorn' yet acknowledges the statue 'there to mark the place' and so the tale ends. The Old Man's scorn should be compared with the response of Crazy Jane, who 'cried tears down'. They express two reactions to the death of the hero, the decay of the world and the final exhaustion of sexual passion and physical beauty.

No other of Yeats's Cuchulain plays seeks to put Cuchulain so clearly in juxtaposition with the twentieth century. The effect is quite startling. If we imagine the cycle as a whole, we see a progression from the remote and eerie *At the Hawk's Well*, broken up by the rather awkward *The Green Helmet* and more conventional *On Baile's Strand*, to the conflict of *The Only Jealousy of Emer* and this final play, where we are brought down to earth, to our own time, just as the hero is finally released in the moment of vision and transformation. That passage towards vision is continued in 'Cuchulain Comforted', where Yeats takes us through the barrier of death into another world.

We may say that, just as Yeats offers the equivalent of two endings to *The Death of Cuchulain*, he offers two final comments on the tragic process as a whole. One, equivalent to the harlot's song, offers us a context, the twentieth-century world, disillusioning and anti-heroic. It is also the context of the everyday, limited and superficial. It relates to the 'rag-and-bone shop of the heart' ('The Circus Animals' Desertion', *CP*, p. 392), the isolated and often desperate starting-point and centre of the tragic protagonist. Frequently this context of frustration, misery and deprivation, where the great are brought low, where the petty and evil triumph, provides an ironical or sceptical strain to Yeats's evocation of ideal and tragic archetype. The second comment on the tragic process is equivalent to Emer's dance, to Cuchulain's final release. This is the image or ideal, the timeless reality which is echoed in all of us, the transcendent moment which is formed whole and freed from the recurring cycles of history. The two ways of vision are interdependent, scorn and rage balancing magnanimity and love.

Finally, the whole cycle of Cuchulain plays shows Yeats's evocation of tragedy as a process in which joy, differentiated from mere happiness, is born not out of escape from the cycles of love and hatred, subjective and objective, torturer and tortured, but from the full expression of personality, by the expense of energy and the exhaustion of every possibility in ceaseless conflict for the truth of vision. That full expression is finally life itself, completed only as we reach death (*L*, p. 922).

Anthony Bradley remarks of this play, and the wider context of tragedy in Yeats, that its resolution

> poses a problem analogous to that raised by tragic plays which demand a Christian interpretation. If one is made to feel that a hero's death is followed by an eternity of bliss, then the play which culminates in his death will not arouse feelings of pity and terror (at least not to the same extent as a play whose universe is amoral). Yeats's world is not Christian of course, but our sense of doom, disaster and defeat is alleviated somewhat because Cuchulain's death, the play makes clear, is succeeded by his transformation into an image of spiritual perfection. And his spirit survives, even if fleetingly, in modern Ireland.[45]

Since the whole of this study has been intent on suggesting the creation by Yeats of an amoral universe, this passage needs some attention, leading us as it does to the poem 'Cuchulain Comforted'. I have already suggested that for Aristotle's fear and pity Yeats substitutes terror and delight. Neither *The Death of Cuchulain* nor 'Cuchulain Comforted' suggests anything resembling 'eternal bliss'. Cuchulain is indeed purified spiritually, but this purification is a purgatorial or cathartic process and leads the hero back through life towards a new incarnation of struggle. There is no final release. Finally, a comparison of Yeatsian tragedy with *Sophocles' Oedipus at Colonus* should make clear that in all tragedy when we can no longer say, 'This is the worst', our doom is finally complete, our last despair ended on an entrance to vision:

> presently they ceased to sob and to cry out and there was silence, and then a voice summoned Oedipus, and the hair

stood up on our heads, for it was a God that spoke. It summoned Oedipus not once but many times. 'Oedipus, Oedipus,' it said, 'what keeps you there? We must set out upon our journey.' (*CPl*, p. 572)

In 'Cuchulain Comforted' (*CP*, pp. 395–6) Yeats takes us as far on the journey of transformation as possible. Cuchulain begins his journey in vigour:

> A man that had six mortal wounds, a man
> Violent and famous, strode among the dead;
> Eyes stared out of the branches and were gone.

His rattle of arms terrifies the muttering and fearful Shrouds of this underworld after-life, but, as he grows still, they creep towards him and initiate him into the process of purgatorial expiation. As Harold Bloom suggests,[46] these Shrouds are passing through the phases or states Yeats depicts in 'The Soul in Judgement'. The exact reverse of the hero, 'Convicted cowards all', there yet seems a bizarre appropriateness in their meeting. Cuchulain's shade consents to follow them, unquestioning. He echoes Yeats's vision of a pure and aimless joy and is led towards a rebirth:

> 'Now we must sing and sing the best we can . . . .'
> They sang, but had not human tunes nor words,
> Though all was done in common as before;

> They had changed their throats and had the throats
>   of birds.

We are left, then, with wordless song and flight into the unknown. We recall Yeats's comments in his Preface to *Cuchulain of Muirthemne*:

> The characters must remain the same, but the strength of Fergus may change so greatly that he, who a moment before was merely a strong man among many, becomes the master of Three Blows that would destroy an army, did they not cut off the heads of three little hills instead, and his sword, which a fool had been able to steal out of its sheath, has of a sudden the likeness of the rainbow.[47]

Yeats returns simultaneously to the themes of enchantment and magical transformation which first delighted him in Irish legends and folktales. We are left with a sense of surprise, a surprise which is akin to delighted wonder. Who, recalling O'Grady's 'It is that famous man Cuchulain', (*VPl*, p. 567), would expect this final outcome for the hero, an outcome which is also a beginning?

I should like to conclude this discussion of Yeats's tragic universe by summing up its most distinctive features. The first of these is its remarkable coherence, remarkable because of its range. From the hero of the early poem 'Cuchulain's Fight with the Sea' (*CP*, pp. 37–40), to the exploration and creation of *A Vision's* world system – in which civilisations are spread beneath our feet in an endless and inescapable process of birth and death; from the tortured figures of Oedipus, Swift and the Old Man of *Purgatory* – the tale returns to the lonely figure of Cuchulain facing death. Throughout we are conscious of ironies, twists of fate and, above all, conflict, exhilaration, and the impetus towards an intense vision which is both self-destructive and a re-creation of the self.

There are many ways of describing the tragic condition in which Yeats sees man dwell, the condition in which 'Man is in love and loves what vanishes'. In an article critical of the later Yeats, Denis Donoghue comments that Yeats was 'intensely and often painfully preoccupied with the war of Soul and Body'. This war is only one expression of Yeatsian tragedy. But Donoghue's use of the words 'intensely' and 'painfully' does sum up the Yeatsian hero's double vision of ecstatic desire and horrified frustration of desire. Donoghue perceives that the quest for 'wholeness, unity, perfection' is 'in the nature of the case . . . constantly the goad of its own despair'.[48] Yet later, or so it seems to me, Donoghue fails to understand Yeats's quest for intensity, commenting, 'The trouble was that he could not value the human body in itself; only when it agreed to wear a bright halo of animation'.[49] The nature of Yeats's world is its hopeless thrusting after a 'bright halo', its doomed search for ecstatic visionary splendour.

Yeats's tragic world, with all its gaiety, its tragic joy, its moments of wonder and miracle, is shot through with darkness. It is a bleak vision and it leaves the way open only for tragic struggle, conflict with the night. This is not a popular vision.

One searching judgement of Yeats is found in Francis Stuart's *Black List, Section H*, and I finish with it. Stuart's H expresses a mingled jealousy of, and admiration for the poet. In H's own aspirations I see echoes both of Yeats's friends in the 1890s, his 'tragic generation', and of much in Yeats's later poetry and plays. For H, the poets (and novelists) of the future

> would be drawn toward ever greater areas of solitude from which they were unlikely to bring back the sort of news that would be greeted with applause. . . . H had an inkling that his concept was valid for the days that were coming, and that Yeats belonged to the last of the great writers whose vision could still be contained within the moral and cultural structure of their time. Later, there were occasions when it struck H that Yeats was not unaware of this and that, playing with the idea of revolt and disruption, he adopted certain extreme attitudes which weren't spontaneous.[50]

I should modify Stuart's judgement thus: Yeats was but barely contained within the structure of his time; while the lack of spontaneity can be seen, as Yeats earlier saw the struggle of Swift and Blake, as a straining towards a new and difficult vision of 'the desolation of reality'.

Notes

INTRODUCTION

1. William Blake, *Complete Writings*, ed. G. Keynes (London: Oxford University Press, 1966) p. 217.
2. Helen Vendler, *Yeats's 'Vision' and the Later Plays* (Cambridge, Mass.: Harvard University Press, 1963).
3. Balachandra Rajan in 'Yeats, Synge and the Tragic Understanding', *Theatre and the Visual Arts: A Centenary Celebration of Jack Yeats and John Synge*, Yeats Studies no. 2, ed. Robert O'Driscoll and Lorna Reynolds (Dublin: Irish University Press, 1972) p. 69.
4. Ibid.
5. Ibid., p. 72.
6. Ibid., p. 71.
7. Ibid., p. 69.
8. Ibid., p. 72.
9. Ibid.
10. Harold Bloom, *Yeats* (New York: Oxford University Press, 1970).
11. Jan Kott, *The Eating of the Gods: An Interpretation of Greek Tragedy*, tr. Boleslaw Taborski and Edward Czerwinski (London: Eyre Methuen, 1974) pp. ix–x.
12. Ibid., p. xviii.
13. Ibid., p. x.
14. Murray Krieger, *The Tragic Vision* (New York: Holt, Reinhart and Winston, 1960) p. 20.
15. Ibid., pp. 30–1.

CHAPTER 1. CUCHULAIN AND THE SIDHE: VISION AND TRAGIC ENCOUNTER

1. Yeats, Preface to Augusta Gregory, *Cuchulain of Muirthemne. The Story of the Men of the Red Branch of Ulster* (Gerrard's Cross, Bucks: Colin Smythe, 1970) p. 15.
2. Yeats, in *Davis, Mangan, Ferguson: Tradition and the Irish Writer*, Tower series of Anglo-Irish Studies II (Dublin: Dolmen Press, 1970) p. 47.

3. Ibid., p. 46.
4. Ibid., p. 47.
5. Ibid.
6. Ibid., p. 50.
7. Ibid., p. 51.
8. Ibid.
9. Ibid.
10. Vendler, *Yeats's 'Vision' and the Later Plays*, p. 236.
11. Ibid.
12. See Bloom, who comments, 'Cuchulain is the hero in his glory, yet already in decline' (*Yeats*, p. 153).
13. Yeats, *The Celtic Twilight* (Gerrard's Cross, Bucks: Colin Smythe, 1981).
14. Ibid., pp. 153–4.
15. Ibid., p. 154.
16. Ibid., p. 155.
17. Yeats, Preface to Gregory, *Cuchulain of Muirthemne*, pp. 11–17.
18. Ibid., p. 12.
19. Ibid.
20. Ibid.
21. Ibid., p. 13.
22. Ibid., p. 14.
23. Ibid., p. 15.
24. Ibid., p. 13.
25. Ibid., p. 16.
26. Yeats's development as a playwright and his experiments with new theatre techniques are well chronicled in James Flannery's *W. B. Yeats and the Idea of a Theatre: The Early Abbey Theatre in Theory and Practice* (New Haven, Conn., and London: Yale University Press, 1976). Flannery is one of the few critics to examine Yeats's plays as theatre and to see Yeats's innovations in the context of contemporary theatre development. Of particular interest in Flannery's discussion is Yeats's relationship with Gordon Craig (pp. 245–54, 262–72).
27. Reg Skene in *The Cuchulain Plays of W. B. Yeats: A Study* (London: Macmillan, 1974) defines the battle between Aoife and Cuchulain as between sun and moon, 'a wheel of love and hate' (p. 39). Skene detects many correspondences between the Cuchulain cycle and Yeats's phases of the moon as well as correspondences with ancient Celtic festivals. Thus *On Baile's Strand* falls at phase twelve of Yeats's system (p. 52). In this system the final play, *The Death of Cuchulain*, falls in phase twenty-two, which is the summer solstice, 'after which the sun begins to lose its battle with the forces of darkness' and when 'the solar year has run its course' (p.

59). Skene's identification of the Cuchulain cycle with ancient ritual is interesting but outside the scope of my study.

28.   L. E. Nathan, *The Tragic Drama of W. B. Yeats* (New York and London: Columbia University Press, 1965) p. 7.
29.   Dennis Donoghue, *Yeats*, Fontana Modern Masters (London, Fontana, 1976) p. 100.
30.   J. M. Synge, *Collected Works*, IV (*Plays*, II), ed. Ann Saddlemyer (London: Oxford University Press, 1968) p. 267.
31.   See also Richard Fallis, '"I Seek an Image": The Method of Yeats's Criticism', *Modern Language Quarterly*, XXXVII, no. 1 (Mar 1976) 72. Fallis comments on Yeats's criticism as 'an attempt to make the reader see what exists in the critic's own inner eyes'. Thus Blake is visualised as 'a man chained in his mythology', Shelley seen 'in a Neoplatonic landscape of caverns, streams and stars', while 'J. M. Synge is a rocky apocalyptic landscape'.
32.   Rajan, in *Theatre and the Visual Arts*, p. 71 and pp. 69–73 *passim*.
33.   Ibid., p. 69.
34.   Ibid., p. 72.
35.   Flannery also argues that this omission is a serious flaw in the play and that 'while theatrically effective *Deirdre* fails to evoke the full intensity and resonance of Yeatsian tragedy' (*Yeats and the Idea of a Theatre*, p. 46).
36.   Anthony Bradley, in *William Butler Yeats*, World Dramatist series (New York: Ungar, 1979), quotes from a director of the play 'who found it "well-nigh unstageable in any acceptable dramatic idiom" and tended to clash with the mood and content of other Cuchulain plays' (p. 201).
37.   Vendler, *Yeats's 'Vision' and the Later Plays*, p. 203.

CHAPTER 2.   THE LANDSCAPE OF TRAGEDY: THREE DANCE PLAYS

1.   Nathan, *The Tragic Drama of W. B. Yeats*, p. 7.
2.   Ibid., p. 13.
3.   Ibid.
4.   Barton R. Friedman, *Adventures in the Deeps of the Mind: The Cuchulain Cycle of W. B. Yeats* (Princeton, NJ: Princeton University Press, 1977) p. 8.
5.   Ibid., p. 9.
6.   Ibid., p. 14.
7.   Ibid., p. 13.
8.   Ibid., p. 12.
9.   Richard Taylor, *Irish Myth and the Japanese Nō* (New Haven, Conn.: Yale University Press, 1966) p. 119.

10. Vendler, *Yeats's 'Vision' and the Later Plays*, p. 194.
11. Vendler (ibid., pp. 254–255) refers us to T. S. Eliot's *After Strange Gods: A Primer of Modern Heresy* (London: Faber, 1934) pp. 45–6, where he quotes this passage.
12. An interesting study of Yeats and the Japanese Noh theatre is offered in Akhtar Qamber's study *Yeats and the Noh: With Two Plays for Dancers by Yeats and Two Noh Plays* (New York: Weatherhill, 1974). Of particular interest is his description of Noh plays in performance (pp. 51–5). Qamber speaks throughout with great enthusiasm as a devotee of the Noh theatre, but he concludes that Yeats's experiment ultimately fails because of 'the absence (in the West) of centuries of tradition, both social and artistic' (p. 112). Finally, 'The Noh plays of Japan and Yeats's plays for dancers are brilliant spots of eccentricity in theatre' (p. 114).
13. Donoghue, *Yeats*, p. 104.
14. David R. Clark, *W. B. Yeats and the Theatre of Desolate Reality* (Dublin: Dolmen Press, 1965) p. 47.
15. Ibid., p. 59.
16. Bloom, *Yeats*, p. 297.
17. Vendler, *Yeats's 'Vision' and the Later Plays*, pp. 206, 208 and 213–14.
18. Ibid., p. 206 and pp. 206–16 *passim*.
19. Ibid., p. 211.
20. Bloom, *Yeats*, p. 296.
21. Vendler, *Yeats's 'Vision' and the Later Plays*, p. 219.
22. Bloom, *Yeats*, p. 301.
23. Qamber comments perceptively that 'The villain is within. It is not really Bricriu. Yeats has presented an inner conflict symbolically' (*Yeats and the Noh*, pp. 90–1).
24. The stage directions are the same for both versions of the play.
25. Clark, *Yeats and the Theatre of Desolate Reality*, p. 45.
26. *Certain Noble Plays of Japan*, from the manuscripts of Ernest Fenellosa, chosen and finished by Ezra Pound, with an introduction by W. B. Yeats (Dublin: Cuala, 1916; facsimile by Irish University Press, 1971) pp. 1–16.
27. Clark, *Yeats and the Theatre of Desolate Reality*, p. 54.
28. It is a Swedenborgian hell. See *E*, p. 37.
29. Taylor, *Irish Myth and the Japanese Nō*, p. 62.
30. Ibid., p. 66.
31. Ibid., p. 52.
32. This is of course stated most definitively in *Letters on Poetry from W. B. Yeats to Dorothy Wellesley*, ed. Dorothy Wellesley (London: Oxford University Press, 1940) p. 9. Yeats describes a gift of lapis lazuli, remarking that 'the east has its solutions always and therefore knows nothing of tragedy. It is we, not the east, that must raise the heroic cry'.

CHAPTER 3. A TRAGIC UNIVERSE: THE FRAMEWORK OF *A VISION*

1. Vendler, *Yeats's 'Vision' and the Later Plays*, p. vii.
2. Thomas Whitaker, *Swan and Shadow: Yeats's Dialogue with History* (Chapel Hill: University of North Carolina Press, 1964).
3. Bloom, *Yeats*, pp. 174–5.
4. Vendler, *Yeats's 'Vision' and the Later Plays*, *passim*.
5. Ibid., p. 30.
6. Ibid.
7. Giorgio Melchiori, *The Whole Mystery of Art: Pattern into Poetry in the Work of W. B. Yeats* (London: Routledge and Kegan Paul, 1960) p. 56.
8. Ibid.
9. Bloom, *Yeats*, p. 217.
10. Vendler, *Yeats's 'Vision' and the Later Plays*, p. 41.
11. Bloom, *Yeats*, p. 211.
12. Whitaker, *Swan and Shadow*, p. 4.
13. Ibid.
14. Ibid.
15. Ibid., p. 6.
16. Ibid.
17. Ibid., p. 7.
18. Ibid., p. 8.
19. Ibid., p. 50.
20. Ibid., p. 52.
21. Ibid., p. 53.
22. Ibid., p. 54.
23. Ibid.
24. Ibid.
25. Ibid.
26. Ibid.
27. Ibid.
28. Bloom, *Yeats*, p. 212.
29. Ibid., p. 211.
30. Ibid.
31. Ibid., p. 212.
32. Ibid., p. 216. Bloom quotes from *The Works of William Blake, Poetic, Symbolic, and Critical*, ed. W. B. Yeats and E. J. Ellis, 3 vols (London: Quaritch, 1893) I, 242.
33. Bloom, *Yeats*, p. 216.
34. Ibid., p. 218.
35. Ibid.
36. Ibid.

37. Ibid., p. 220.
38. Ibid.
39. Ibid., p. 222.
40. Ibid., p. 223.
41. Ibid., p. 230.
42. Ibid., p. 234.
43. Ibid.
44. Whitaker, *Swan and Shadow*, p. 50.
45. Bloom, *Yeats*, p. 253.
46. Ibid., pp. 253–4.
47. Ibid., p. 254.
48. Ibid.
49. Ibid., p. 219.
50. Donoghue, *Yeats*, p. 83.
51. Sophocles, *Antigone*, in *The Theban Plays*, tr. E. F. Watling (Harmondsworth: Penguin, 1974) p. 153.
52. Blake, *Complete Writings*, p. 290.
53. Harold Bloom, in *Blake: A Collection of Critical Essays*, ed. Northrop Frye (Englewood Cliffs, NJ: Prentice-Hall, 1966) p. 109.
54. George Steiner, *The Death of Tragedy* (London: Faber, 1963) p. 124.
55. Bloom, *Yeats*, p. 218.
56. Steiner, *The Death of Tragedy*, p. 127.
57. Blake, *Complete Writings*, p. 210.
58. Kott, *The Eating of the Gods*, pp. ix–x.
59. Corinna Salvadori, *Yeats and Castiglione: Poet and Courtier* (Dublin: Figgis, 1965) pp. 19–20.
60. Ibid., p. 4.
61. Ibid.
62. Ibid., p. 8.
63. Ibid., pp. 10–11.
64. Nietzsche, *The Birth of Tragedy and the Case of Wagner*, tr. Walter Kaufmann (New York: Random House, Vintage Books, 1967) p. 33.
65. Ibid., pp. 35–6.
66. Ibid., p. 39.
67. Blake, *Complete Writings*, pp. 425–7.
68. Nietzsche, *The Birth of Tragedy*, p. 74.
69. Ibid., p. 104.
70. Ibid., p. 17.
71. Ibid., pp. 17–18.
72. Ibid., p. 24.
73. Ibid., p. 26.
74. Donoghue, in *Yeats*, pp. 55–6, quotes from Nietzsche's *The Will to Power*, tr. Walter Kaufmann and R. J. Hollingdale (London:

Weidenfield and Nicolson, 1968) p. 346.
75. Ibid.
76. See also *V*, pp. 207–8, for Yeats's commentary on the significance of the Sphinx and the Buddha.
77. Vendler, *Yeats's 'Vision' and the Later Plays*, pp. 22–5.
78. Ibid., p. 24.
79. This passage is quoted in Vendler, ibid.
80. Ibid.
81. T. R. Henn, *The Lonely Tower: Studies in the Poetry of W. B. Yeats* (London: Methuen, 1965) pp. 256–7.
82. Vendler, *Yeats's 'Vision' and the Later Plays*, p. 211.
83. *The Variorum Edition of the Poems of W. B. Yeats*, ed. Peter Allt and Russell K. Alspach (London: Macmillan, 1973) p. 825.
84. Jon Stallworthy, *Between the Lines* (Oxford: Clarendon Press, 1963) p. 21.
85. In 'The Mother of God' (*CP*, pp. 281–2), however, Yeats's treatment of the Christian myth is marked by a gentleness of tone rare in his work.
86. Vendler, *Yeats's 'Vision' and the Later Plays*, p. 106.
87. Ibid., p. 107.
88. Ibid.
89. Whitaker, *Swan and Shadow*, p. 182.
90. Ibid.
91. Ibid.
92. Ibid., p. 183.
93. '"Man can embody Truth, but he cannot know it." I must embody it in the completion of my life' (*L*, p. 922).

CHAPTER 4.   FOUR PLAYS AND THE PROBLEM OF EVIL

1. Whitaker, *Swan and Shadow*, p. 131.
2. Ibid., p. 50.
3. Martin Buber, *Eclipse of God: Studies in the Relation between Religion and Philosophy* (New York: Harper, 1957) p. 87; quoted in Whitaker, *Swan and Shadow*, p. 50.
4. Ibid., p. 52.
5. Ibid., p. 53.
6. Vendler, *Yeats's 'Vision' and the Later Plays*, p. 41.
7. Ibid.
8. See particularly *A*, p. 273, and *M*, p. 328.
9. Vendler, *Yeats's 'Vision' and the Later Plays*, pp. 71–90.
10. Ibid., p. 41.

11. Ibid., p. 100.
12. Ibid.
13. A. C. Bradley, *Oxford Lectures on Poetry* (London: Macmillan, 1959) p. 71.
14. Ibid.
15. Ibid., p. 84.
16. Ibid., p. 85.
17. T. R. Henn, *The Harvest of Tragedy* (London: Methuen, 1966) pp. 65–71.
18. Ibid., p. 66.
19. Ibid., p. 67.
20. Ibid., p. 68.
21. James Thompson, 'City of Dreadul Night', *Poems of Faith and Doubt: The Victorian Age*, ed. R. L. Brett (London: Edward Arnold, 1965) p. 170; quoted in Henn, *The Harvest of Tragedy*, p. 68.
22. Ibid., p. 68.
23. Paul Tillich, *The Shaking of the Foundations* (Harmondsworth: Penguin, 1962) pp. 27–9.
24. Ibid., p. 31.
25. Ibid., p. 44.
26. Ibid., p. 28.
27. Ibid.
28. Vendler, *Yeats's 'Vision' and the Later Plays*, pp. 103–4.
29. Yeats here records an oral version of the tale in preference to the more elaborate version to be found in *The Works of Oscar Wilde* (London: Collins, 1948) pp. 843–4.
30. Whitaker, *Swan and Shadow*, pp. 43–6. See also F. A. C. Wilson, *Yeats's Iconography* (London: Gollancz, 1960) pp. 173–4.
31. Whitaker, *Swan and Shadow*, pp. 44–5.
32. *The New Catholic Encyclopaedia*, IX (New York: McGraw-Hill, 1967) pp. 184–5.
33. Vendler, *Yeats's 'Vision' and the Later Plays*, p. 109.
34. Ibid., p. 254.
35. Ibid., p. 110.
36. Ibid., pp. 110–11.
37. Whitaker, *Swan and Shadow*, pp. 94–5.
38. Bradley, *William Butler Yeats*, p. 223.
39. Ibid., p. 224.
40. Vendler, *Yeats's 'Vision' and the Later Plays*, p. 182.
41. Whitaker, *Swan and Shadow*, p. 106.
42. Ibid., p. 107.
43. Jonathan Swift, *A Tale of the Tubs, with Other Early Works, 1696–707*, ed. Herbert Davis (Oxford: Blackwell, 1939) p. 228.
44. See ibid., p. 228:

For, though we cannot prolong the period of a commonwealth beyond the decree of heaven, or the date of its nature, any more than human life beyond the strength of the seminal virtue; yet we may manage a sickly constitution, and preserve a strong one; we may watch and prevent accidents . . . and by these and other such methods, render a state long-lived, though not immortal.

45. Douglas N. Archibald, 'Yeats's Encounter with Jonathan Swift', in *Yeats and the Theatre*, Yeats Studies no. 1, ed. Robert O'Driscoll and Lorna Reynolds (London: Macmillan, 1975) p. 198.
46. Ibid., p. 199.
47. Ibid., p. 213.
48. Clark, *Yeats and the Theatre of Desolate Reality*, p. 61.
49. Ibid., p. 62.
50. Ibid., pp. 63–5.
51. Ibid., pp. 83–4.
52. Ibid., pp. 82–3.
53. Ibid.
54. Donald Torchiana, in *W. B. Yeats and Georgian Ireland* (Evanston, Ill.: Northwestern University Press, 1966) p. 127, refers both to this letter and to a passage in *Autobiographies* (p. 330) where Yeats again describes 'these holy victims'. He talks of psychical research offering evidence to support legends about saints who 'did really cure disease by taking it upon themselves. As disease was considered the consequence of sin, to take it upon themselves was to copy Christ.'
55. Richard Ellmann, *Yeats, The Man and the Masks* (London: Oxford University Press, 1979) p. 201. (First published 1949.)
56. Jonathan Swift, *Gulliver's Travels* (Harmondsworth: Penguin, 1979) p. 315.
57. Ibid., p. 339.
58. Torchiana, *Yeats and Georgian Ireland*, pp. 135–7.
59. F. A. Lucas, *The Drama of Chekhov, Synge, Yeats and Pirandello* (London: Cassell, 1963) pp. 337–9.
60. Vendler, *Yeats's 'Vision' and the Later Plays*, p. 195.
61. Peter Ure, *Yeats the Playwright: A Commentary on Character and Design in the Major Plays* (London: Routledge and Kegan Paul, 1963) p. 107.
62. Ibid.
63. Ibid.

CONCLUSION: THE DEATH OF THE HERO

1. Skene, *The Cuchulain Plays*, pp. 222–40.
2. F. A. C. Wilson, *Yeats and Tradition* (London: Gollancz, 1959) p. 163.
3. Ure, *Yeats the Playwright*, p. 78.
4. Bloom, *Yeats*, p. 430. (He is referring to Helen Vendler's discussion of the play in *Yeats's 'Vision' and the Later Plays*, p. 240.)
5. Ure, *Yeats the Playwright*, p. 82.
6. Ibid.
7. Bloom, *Yeats*, p. 430.
8. Ibid., p. 429.
9. Ibid., p. 430.
10. Ibid.
11. Ure, *Yeats the Playwright*, p. 80.
12. Ibid.
13. Ibid., p. 81.
14. Ibid.
15. Ibid., p. 82.
16. Ibid., p. 81.
17. 'According to Rilke a man's death is born with him and if his life is successful and he escapes mere "mass death" his nature is completed by his final union with it. Rilke gives Hamlet's death as an example' (*L*, p. 917).
18. Ure, *Yeats the Playwright*, p. 82.
19. Bloom, *Yeats*, p. 431.
20. Gregory, *Cuchulain of Muirthemne*, p. 252.
21. Ibid., p. 256.
22. Ibid., p. 259.
23. Ibid.
24. Ibid., p. 263.
25. Yeats, in *Davis, Mangan, Ferguson: Tradition and the Irish Writer*, pp. 48–53.
26. Ibid., p. 50.
27. Ibid.
28. Ibid.
29. Ibid.
30. Ibid., p. 51.
31. Ibid.
32. Vendler, *Yeats's 'Vision' and the Later Plays*, pp. 237–8.
33. Ibid., p. 238.
34. Skene, *The Cuchulain Plays*, p. 225.
35. Skene (ibid., p. 226) identifies the dancer as Ninette de Valois performing as Fand in *The Only Jealousy of Emer*.

36. See Rajan, in *Theatre and the Visual Arts*, ed. O'Driscoll and Reynolds, p. 71.

37. Skene, *The Cuchulain Plays*, p. 236.

38. Bloom, *Yeats*, p. 430.

39. Ibid.

40. Ibid., p. 432.

41. Ure, *Yeats the Playwright*, p. 78.

42. Skene, *The Cuchulain Plays*, p. 226.

43. Ure, *Yeats the Playwright*, p. 78.

44. Skene, *The Cuchulain Plays*, p. 239.

45. Bradley, *William Butler Yeats*, p. 190.

46. Bloom, *Yeats*, p. 464.

47. Yeats, Preface to Gregory, *Cuchulain of Muirthemne*, pp. 14–15.

48. Denis Donoghue, 'The Human Image in Yeats', in *Irish University Review*, III, no. 8 (1966) 56.

49. Ibid., p. 63.

50. Francis Stuart, *Black List, Section H* (London: Martin Brian and O'Keefe, 1975) p. 122. See also p. 44, where Stuart comments,

> He believed that nothing short of the near despair of being utterly cast off from society and its principles could create the inner condition conducive to the new insights that it was the task of the poet to reveal. . . . Yeats, for all his superb craftsmanship and intellectual passion, was not going to cause any real alteration or reorientation in inner attitudes because he had not been forced to the point of extreme loneliness.

> Such a reorientation of inner attitudes, such despair and loneliness is, I should argue, the hallmark of the later Yeats and reaches its climax in *The Words upon the Window-Pane* and *Purgatory*.

Bibliography

A. WORKS BY YEATS

(i) *Books by and editions of Yeats*

Ah, Sweet Dancer. W. B. Yeats, Margot Ruddock: A Correspondence, ed. Roger McHugh (London: Macmillan, 1970).
Autobiographies (London: Macmillan, 1955).
The Celtic Twilight (Gerrards Cross, Bucks: Colin Smythe, 1981).
The Collected Plays of W. B. Yeats, 2nd edn (London: Macmillan, 1952).
The Collected Poems of W. B. Yeats, 2nd edn (London: Macmillan, 1950).
The Correspondence of Robert Bridges and W. B. Yeats, ed. Richard J. Finneran (London: Macmillan, 1977).
A Critical Edition of 'A Vision', ed. George Mills Harper and Walter Kelly Hood (London: Macmillan, 1978). (First published 1925.)
Davis, Mangan, Ferguson: Tradition and the Irish Writer (with Thomas Kinsella), Tower Series of Anglo-Irish Studies II (Dublin: Dolmen Press, 1970).
Essays and Introductions (London: Macmillan, 1961).
Explorations (London: Macmillan, 1962).
The Letters of W. B. Yeats, ed. Allan Wade (London: Rupert Hart-Davis, 1954).
Letters on Poetry from W. B. Yeats to Dorothy Wellesley, ed. Dorothy Wellesley (London: Oxford University Press, 1940).
Mythologies (London: Macmillan, 1959).
The Senate Speeches of W. B. Yeats, ed. Donald R. Pearce (Bloomington: Indiana University Press, 1960).
The Variorum Edition of the Poems of W. B. Yeats, ed. Peter Allt and Russell K. Alspach (London: Macmillan, 1957).
The Variorum Edition of the Plays of W. B. Yeats, ed. Russell K. Alspach (London: Macmillan, 1966).
A Vision (London: Macmillan, 1962). (First published 1937.)
W. B. Yeats and T. Sturge Moore: Their Correspondence 1901–1937, ed. Ursula Bridge (London: Routledge and Kegan Paul, 1953).

(ii) *Articles, prefaces, introductions and works edited by Yeats*

Carleton, William, *Stories from Carleton*, ed. W. B. Yeats (New York: Lemma, 1973). (First published 1889.)

Fenellosa, Ernest, *Certain Noble Plays of Japan*, from the manuscripts of Ernest Fenellosa, chosen and finished by Ezra Pound, with an introduction by W. B. Yeats (Dublin: Cuala, 1916; facsimile by Irish University Press, 1971).

Gregory, Augusta, *Cuchulain of Muirthemne. The Story of the Men of the Red Branch of Ulster*, arranged and put into English by Lady Gregory, with a Preface by W. B. Yeats (Gerrards Cross, Bucks: Colin Smythe, 1970). (First published 1902.)

The Oxford Book of Modern Verse, ed. and intro. W. B. Yeats (Oxford: Clarendon Press, 1936).

The Works of William Blake, Poetic, Symbolic and Critical, ed. W. B. Yeats and E. J. Ellis (London: Quaritch, 1893) 3 vols.

Yeats, W. B., 'The New Irish Library', *Bookman* (London), June 1896.

B. GENERAL

Blake, William, *The Complete Writings*, ed. G. Keynes (London: Oxford University Press, 1966).

———, *The Poetry and Prose of William Blake*, ed. David V. Erdmann (New York: Doubleday, 1965).

———, *The Works of William Blake, Poetic, Symbolic, and Critical. See under* A (ii).

Blake: A Collection of Critical Essays, ed. Northrop Frye (Englewood Cliffs, NJ: Prentice-Hall, 1966).

Bradley, A. C., *Oxford Lectures on Poetry* (London: Macmillan, 1959).

Buber, Martin, *The Eclipse of God: Studies in the Relation between Religion and Philosophy* (New York: Harper, 1957).

———, *I and Thou* (New York: Harper, 1958).

Carleton, William, *Stories from Carleton. See under* A (ii).

Castiglione, Baldassarre, *The Book of the Courtier*, tr. George Bull (Harmondsworth: Penguin, 1976).

Corkery, Daniel, *Synge and Anglo-Irish Literature* (Cork: Cork University Press, 1931).

Costello, Peter, *The Heart Grown Brutal: The Irish Revolution in Literature, from Parnell to the Death of Yeats, 1891–1939* (Dublin: Gill and Macmillan, 1977).

Eliot, T. S., *After Strange Gods: A Primer of Modern Heresy*, the Page-Barbour Lectures at the University of Virginia 1933 (London: Faber, 1934).

Gregory, Augusta, *Cuchulain of Muirthemne. See under* A (ii).

Henn, Thomas Rice, *The Harvest of Tragedy* (London: Methuen, 1966).
Irish Poets in English, Thomas Davis Lectures, ed. Sean Lucy (Dublin and Cork: Mercier, 1973).
Kinsella, Thomas, *Davis, Mangan, Ferguson: Tradition and the Irish Writer. See under* A (i).
Kott, Jan, *The Eating of the Gods: An Interpretation of Greek Tragedy*, tr. Boleslaw Taborski and Edward J. Czerwinski (London: Eyre Methuen, 1974).
Krieger, Murray, *The Tragic Vision* (New York: Holt, Reinhart and Winston, 1960).
Nietzsche, Friedrich, *Beyond Good and Evil*, tr. R. J. Hollingdale (Harmondsworth: Penguin, 1981).
_____, *The Birth of Tragedy and The Case of Wagner*, tr. Walter Kaufmann (New York: Random House, Vintage Books, 1967).
_____, *The Will to Power*, tr. Walter Kaufmann and R. J. Hollingdale (London: Weidenfield and Nicolson, 1968).
Poems of Faith and Doubt: The Victorian Age, ed. R. L. Brett (London: Edward Arnold, 1965).
Sophocles, *The Theban Plays*, tr. E. F. Watling (Harmondsworth: Penguin, 1974).
Steiner, George, *The Death of Tragedy* (London: Faber, 1963).
Stuart, Francis, *Black List, Section H* (London: Martin Brian and O'Keefe, 1975).
Swift, Jonathan, *Gulliver's Travels* (Harmondsworth: Penguin, 1979).
_____, *A Tale of a Tub, with Other Early Works 1696–1707*, ed. Herbert Davis (Oxford: Blackwell, 1939).
_____, *Works*, ed. R. B. Sheridan (London, 1784).
Synge, John Millington, *Collected Works*, IV (*Plays*, II), ed. Ann Saddlemyer (London: Oxford University Press, 1968).
Tillich, Paul, *The Shaking of the Foundations* (Harmondsworth: Penguin, 1962).
Wilde, Oscar, *The Works of Oscar Wilde* (London: Collins, 1948).

C. BOOKS ON YEATS

Bloom, Harold, *Yeats* (New York: Oxford University Press, 1970).
Bohlmann, Otto, *Yeats and Nietzsche: An Exploration of Major Nietzschean Echoes in the Writings of William Butler Yeats* (London: Macmillan, 1982).
Bradford, Curtis, *Yeats at Work* (Carbondale: Southern Illinois University Press, 1965).
_____, *Yeats's Last Poems Again*, Yeats Centenary Papers no. VIII (Dublin: Dolmen Press, 1966).

Bradley, Anthony, *William Butler Yeats*, World Dramatist series (New York: Ungar, 1979).

Clark, David R., *W. B. Yeats and the Theatre of Desolate Reality* (Dublin: Dolmen Press, 1965).

Cullingford, Elizabeth, *Yeats, Ireland and Fascism* (London: Macmillan, 1981).

Donoghue, Denis, *Yeats*, Fontana Modern Masters (London: Fontana, 1976).

Dyson, A. E., *Yeats, Eliot and R. S. Thomas* (London: Macmillan 1981).

Ellmann, Richard, *The Identity of Yeats* (London: Faber, 1964). (First published 1954.)

——, *Yeats: The Man and the Masks* (London: Oxford University Press, 1979). (First published 1949.)

Flannery, James W., *W. B. Yeats and the Idea of a Theatre: The Early Abbey Theatre in Theory and Practice* (New Haven, Conn., and London: Yale University Press, 1976).

Friedman, Barton R., *Adventures in the Deeps of the Mind: The Cuchulain Cycle of W. B. Yeats* (Princeton, NJ: Princeton University Press, 1977).

Henn, Thomas Rice, *Last Essays* (Gerrards Cross, Bucks: Colin Smythe, 1976).

——, *The Lonely Tower: Studies in the Poetry of W. B. Yeats* (London: Methuen, 1965).

Hirschberg, Stuart, *At the Top of the Tower: Yeats's Poetry Explored through 'A Vision'* (Heidelberg: Carl Winter, 1979).

Hone, Joseph, *W. B. Yeats 1865–1939* (London: Macmillan, 1942).

An Honoured Guest: New Essays on W. B. Yeats, ed. Denis Donoghue and J. R. Mulryne (London: Edward Arnold, 1965).

In Excited Reverie, ed. A. N. Jeffares and K. W. G. Cross (London: Macmillan, 1965).

Jeffares, A. N., *A Commentary on the Collected Poems of W. B. Yeats* (London: Macmillan, 1968).

——, *W. B. Yeats, Man and Poet* (London: Routledge and Kegan Paul, 1949).

—— and Knowland, A. S., *A Commentary on the Collected Plays of W. B. Yeats* (London: Macmillan, 1975).

Kermode, Frank, *Romantic Image* (London: Fontana, 1971). (First published 1957.)

Koch, Vivienne, *The Tragic Phase: A Study of the Last Poems* (London: Routledge and Kegan Paul, 1951).

Lucas, F. A., *The Drama of Chekhov, Synge, Yeats and Pirandello* (London: Cassell, 1963).

Lynch, David, *Yeats: The Poetics of the Self* (Chicago: Chicago University Press, 1979).

Melchiori, Giorgio, *The Whole Mystery of Art: Pattern into Poetry in the Work of W. B. Yeats* (London: Routledge and Kegan Paul, 1960).

Miller, Liam, *The Noble Drama of W. B. Yeats* (Dublin: Dolmen Press, 1977).

Myth and Reality in Irish Literature, ed. Joseph Ronsley (Ontario: Wilfred Laurier University Press, 1977).

Nathan, L. E., *The Tragic Drama of W. B. Yeats* (New York and London: Columbia University Press, 1965).

Parkinson, Thomas, *W. B. Yeats: The Later Poetry* (Berkeley, Calif., and Los Angeles: University of California Press, 1964).

Qamber, Akhtar, *Yeats and the Noh, with Two Plays for Dancers by Yeats and Two Noh Plays* (New York: Weatherhill, 1974).

Raine, Kathleen, *Death-in-Life and Life-in-Death: 'Cuchulain Comforted' and 'News for the Delphic Oracle'*, New Yeats Papers VIII (Dublin: Dolmen Press, 1974).

——, *From Blake to 'A Vision'*, New Yeats Papers XVII (Dublin: Dolmen Press, 1979).

Rajan, Balachandra, *W. B. Yeats: A Critical Introduction* (London: Hutchinson, 1965).

Salvadori, Corinna, *Yeats and Castiglione: Poet and Courtier* (Dublin, Figgis, 1965).

Skene, Reg, *The Cuchulain Plays of W. B. Yeats: A Study* (London: Macmillan, 1974).

Stallworthy, Jon, *Between the Lines* (Oxford: Clarendon Press, 1963).

——, *Vision and Revision in Yeats's Last Poems* (Oxford: Clarendon Press, 1969).

Taylor, Richard, *Irish Myth and the Japanese Nō* (New Haven, Conn., and London: Yale University Press, 1966).

Theatre and the Visual Arts: A Centenary Celebration of Jack Yeats and John Synge, Yeats Studies no. 2, ed. Robert O'Driscoll and Lorna Reynolds (Dublin: Irish University Press, 1972).

Torchiana, Donald, *W. B. Yeats and Georgian Ireland* (Evanston: Northwestern University Press, 1966).

Unterecker, John, *A Reader's Guide to W. B. Yeats* (London: Thames and Hudson, 1973).

Ure, Peter, *Yeats the Playwright: A Commentary on Character and Design in the Major Plays* (London: Routledge and Kegan Paul, 1963).

Vendler, Helen, *Yeats's 'Vision' and the Later Plays* (Cambridge, Mass.: Harvard University Press, 1963).

Whitaker, Thomas, *Swan and Shadow: Yeats's Dialogue with History* (Chapel Hill: University of North Carolina Press, 1964).

Wilson, F. A. C., *W. B. Yeats and Tradition* (London: Gollancz, 1958).

——, *Yeats's Iconography* (London: Gollancz, 1960).

Yeats and the Theatre, ed. Robert O'Driscoll and Lorna Reynolds, Yeats Studies no. 1 (London: Macmillan, 1975).

Yeats: Last Poems, Casebook series, ed. Jon Stallworthy (London: Macmillan, 1968).

Yeats, Sligo and Ireland: Essays to Mark the Twenty-First Yeats International

Summer School, ed. A. N. Jeffares (Gerrard Cross, Bucks: Colin Smythe, 1980).

D. MISCELLANEOUS ARTICLES, REVIEWS, LECTURES AND PAMPHLETS

Donoghue, Denis 'The Human Image in Yeats', *Irish University Review*, III, no. 8 (1966) 56–70.
Fallis, Richard, '"I Seek an Image": The Method of Yeats's Criticism', *Modern Language Quarterly*, XXXVII, no. 1 (Mar 1976) 68–81.
Levine, Herbert J., 'Yeats at the Crossroads: The Debate of Self and Anti-Self in "Ego Dominus Tuus"', *Modern Language Quarterly*, XXXIX, no. 2 (June 1978) 132–53.
Powell, Grosvenor E., 'Yeats's Second "Vision": Berkeley, Coleridge, and the Correspondence with Sturge Moore', *Modern Language Review*, LXXVI, part 2 (Apr 1981) 273–90.

Index

'Acre of Grass, An', 135
Aherne, 105–6
'Among School Children', 61, 76,
  102, 134
anarchy, 97; *see also* evil
'Anima Hominis', 37–8, 49, 52,
  60–1, 100
anti-self: Daimon as, 38, 62, 65; in *A
  Vision*, 68
Aoife, 15, 21–2, 24, 140, 142, 146–7
apocalypse, 62, 72–3, 100; *see also
  Vision, A*
Archibald, Douglas N., 122
Aristotle, 152
Asia, 85–6
At the Hawk's Well, 8, 11–12, 31–5,
  39–40, 46, 48, 51–2, 55, 86, 151
Autobiographies, 3, 17, 119, 137

Balzac, Honoré de, 85
beauty, 47–8, 94
Berkeley, George, 119, 121
Blake, William, 3, 60, 70, 73–4, 77,
  155
Blind Man, the, 20, 24, 36, 140–2,
  144, 147–8
Bloom Harold: on context, 39–40;
  on Cuchulain, 44–5, 139–41, 148;
  on *The Only Jealousy of Emer*, 46–7;
  and *A Vision*, 67–8; on the
  Shrouds, 153; *Yeats*, 5, 65, 69–75
Bradley, A. C., 100
Bradley, Anthony, 114, 152
Bricriu, 50
Buber, Martin, 99
Burke, Edmund, 87

Calvary, 9, 97, 103–4, 106–12, 118

Castiglione, Baldassare, 63; *The Book
  of the Courtier*, 75–6
cataclysm *see* apocalypse
Cathleen ni Houlihan, 12, 55
Catholic Encyclopaedia, The, 111
Celtic Twilight, The, 16
Certain Noble Plays of Japan
  (introduction), 35, 145
chorus, 37, 48–9, 133
Christ, 9, 85, 89, 98–9, 103, 106–11,
  114–18; *see also* Christianity
Christianity, 2–3, 9, 89, 101, 103–5,
  139
'Circus Animals' Desertion, The',
  151
Clark, David, *W. B. Yeats and the
  Theatre of Desolate Reality*, 39, 53,
  58, 122–4, 129
'Cold Heaven, The', 3, 63–7, 131
Conchubar, 15, 20–5
conflict *see* tension
Congal, 15, 142–3
Connolly, James, 150
Conrad, Joseph, 6
'Consolation', 98
'Crazy Jane on God', 133, 135
'Crazy Jane on the Mountain', 149
'Crazy Jane Talks with the Bishop',
  134
Cuchulain: dominating Yeats'
  vision, 1; as tragic figure, 2, 40,
  138; as archetypal hero, 7–9, 32,
  41–2, 51, 137–55; and the Sidhe,
  11–31, 37, 98; Friedman on, 33;
  and Fand, 46–52, 129; and
  conflict, 60
'Cuchulain Comforted', 11, 149,
  151–3